HEADLINE SERIES

No. 311   FOREIGN POLICY ASSOCIATION   Summer

The Future Role of NATO

by Joseph I. Coffey

Cover Design: Ed Bohon $5.95

The Author

JOSEPH I. COFFEY has a B.S. from the U.S. Military Academy and a Ph.D. in international relations from Georgetown University. In his Army career, he served in Intelligence, the Plans Division, the Office of the Assistant Secretary of Defense for International Security Affairs and on the White House staff. Following retirement from the Army, he became a consultant to the Arms Control and Disarmament Agency, the Department of Defense and the State Department.

He taught at Carnegie Mellon University, Georgetown and the University of Pittsburgh, from which he retired as Distinguished Service Professor of Public and International Affairs.

Dr. Coffey is the author of some 40 articles and has produced 10 books and monographs on arms control and defense. He is a partner in Interdisciplinary Research Associates, Princeton, NJ.

The Foreign Policy Association

The Foreign Policy Association is a private, nonprofit, nonpartisan educational organization. Its purpose is to stimulate wider interest and more effective participation in, and greater understanding of, world affairs among American citizens. Among its activities is the continuous publication, dating from 1935, of the HEADLINE SERIES. The author is responsible for factual accuracy and for the views expressed. FPA itself takes no position on issues of U.S. foreign policy.

HEADLINE SERIES (ISSN 0017-8780) is published four times a year, Spring, Summer, Fall and Winter, by the Foreign Policy Association, Inc., 470 Park Avenue So., New York, N.Y. 10016. Chairman, Paul B. Ford; President, Noel V. Lateef; Editor in Chief, Nancy Hoepli-Phalon; Senior Editors, Ann R. Monjo and K.M. Rohan; Assistant Editor, Claudia P. Filos. Subscription rates, $20.00 for 4 issues; $35.00 for 8 issues; $50.00 for 12 issues. Single copy price $5.95; double issue $11.25. Discount 25% on 10 to 99 copies; 30% on 100 to 499; 35% on 500 and over. Payment must accompany all orders. Postage and handling: $2.50 for first copy; $.50 each additional copy. Second-class postage paid at New York, NY, and additional mailing offices. POSTMASTER: Send address changes to HEADLINE SERIES, Foreign Policy Association, 470 Park Avenue So., New York, NY 10016. Copyright 1997 by Foreign Policy Association, Inc. Design by K.M. Rohan. Printed at Science Press, Ephrata, Pennsylvania. Summer 1995. Published April 1997.

Library of Congress Catalog Card No. 97-60622
ISBN 0-87124-175-7

Introduction

IN APRIL 1949 the United States joined with Canada and 10 European nations to sign the North Atlantic Treaty. In the preamble to that treaty the signatories indicated:

▶ *their determination to "safeguard the freedom, common heritage and civilization of their peoples, founded on the principles of democracy, individual liberty and the rule of law";*

▶ *their intent "to promote stability and well-being in the North Atlantic area";*

▶ *their resolve "to unite their efforts for collective defense and for the preservation of peace and security."*

And these objectives are still being pursued today.

The mere recitation of these aspirations does not, however, tell us why they were embodied in a treaty and how the members proposed to achieve them, much less what the United States gained that prompted it to enter into an unprecedented peacetime alliance. Nor does it tell us whether the Atlantic alliance is still necessary, or whether the North Atlantic Treaty Organization (NATO), which was formed to implement it, is still relevant. After all, today's world is very different from the one of 1949. In Europe alone, this period has seen first the expansion of Soviet power and then its withdrawal, followed by the dissolution of the Soviet Union itself into its constituent republics; the formal division of Germany into two states and then its unification; the spread of democratic institutions and market economies to countries from which they have long been absent; and the beginnings of today's European Union (EU) with an integrated economic and financial system and perhaps a common foreign and security policy. And finally, since time does not stand still, there is now the question of NATO's future, the roles that it can and should play and how these might or might not serve American interests.

This is the question addressed here. The book opens with a discussion of why NATO was established and what it has become. The author then looks at how the organization functions and how well it has worked. Next he turns to more-substantive matters, beginning with NATO's adaptation to the end of the cold war, continuing with an assessment of what it is doing with respect to enlargement, relations with Russia, interactions with other European security institutions and the conduct of peace-keeping operations. He then analyzes NATO's future mission. In a final chapter, the book examines U.S. policy with respect to the alliance, a question that concerns all countries.

1

The Origins of NATO

T O UNDERSTAND why NATO was formed one must try to envision the Europe of 1949. With the exception of Sweden, Switzerland, Spain and Portugal, the states of Europe were still enfeebled by wartime devastation, striving for economic recovery, attempting to reestablish shattered political institutions, resettle refugees and recover from the second major upheaval in 30 years. In Western Europe those problems were aggravated by feelings of insecurity stemming in part from the internal challenges to democratic institutions posed by Communists and other extremists (as epitomized by the coup in Czechoslovakia in February 1948, which overthrew the democratic government) and in part from external pressures, principally from the Soviet Union. By 1949 the U.S.S.R. had reincorporated the Baltic republics of Latvia, Lithuania and Estonia, had extended its borders scores of miles to the west, and had established firm control over five countries of Central and Eastern Europe (Poland, Czechoslovakia, Hungary, Romania and

Bulgaria). Furthermore, the U.S.S.R. maintained in all of these countries and in the occupied zone of Germany powerful armed forces outnumbering by four or five to one West European forces. Moreover, by 1948, Soviet leader Joseph Stalin had apparently abandoned his wartime cooperation with the West for a policy of opposition marked not only by obstructionism in international organizations and obstreperousness in interallied conferences but by support for guerrilla operations in Greece and elsewhere. Most importantly, in June 1948 Stalin ordered Soviet forces to close all roads between Berlin, located in the Soviet occupation zone of Germany, and the British, French and American zones, thereby denying the Western allies ground access to their troops in West Berlin and blocking the flow of supplies to the people of that enclave.

This multipronged threat to the integrity and independence of the countries of Western Europe did not go unanswered. In 1947 the United States, under the so-called Truman Doctrine, provided economic and military assistance to Greece and Turkey to help, in the words of President Harry S. Truman, "free peoples who are resisting attempted subjugation by armed minorities or by outside pressure." In that same year, U.S. Secretary of State George C. Marshall announced the European Recovery Program (the Marshall Plan), providing economic and technical assistance to those countries of Europe willing to devise and work on a common program for economic reconstruction. And in 1948, five countries of Western Europe (Belgium, Britain, France, Luxembourg and the Netherlands) signed the Brussels Treaty, pledging to strengthen their economic, social and cultural ties and, in the event of an armed attack in Europe on any signatory, to "afford the party so attacked all the military and other aid and assistance in their power." And to implement this pledge, they formed the Brussels Treaty Organization, subsequently renamed the Western European Union (WEU). The Brussels Treaty was subsequently altered in 1955 by a series of protocols that deleted all references to Germany as an aggressor and admitted that country and Italy to the WEU. This, however, was not deemed enough. Just as the eco-

NATO members

Countries that have
joined the
Partnership for Peace

ICELAND

SWEDEN

RUSSIA

NORWAY

FINLAND

ARMENIA ▶
AZERBAIJAN ▶
ESTONIA   GEORGIA ▶
KAZAKHSTAN ▶
LATVIA KYRGYZSTAN ▶
TURKMENISTAN ▶
LITHUANIA UZBEKISTAN ▶

IRELAND

DENMARK

BRITAIN

NETH.

BELARUS

GERMANY POLAND

BELGIUM

LUX.   CZECH REP.

UKRAINE

FRANCE

SLOVAKIA

MOLDOVA

SWITZ. AUSTRIA HUNGARY

SLOVENIA CROATIA   ROMANIA

PORTUGAL

BOS. & HERZ.

BULGARIA

YUGOSLAVIA

SPAIN

ITALY

F.Y.R. MACEDONIA

ALBANIA

TURKEY

GREECE

nomic resources of the countries of Western Europe would not
suffice for recovery, their military capabilities would not suffice for defense. Recognizing this, both Europeans and Americans sought to broaden the Brussels Treaty Organization to include not only other European states (Denmark, Iceland, Italy,
Norway and Portugal) but Canada and the United States. And
on April 4, 1949, these 12 countries signed the North Atlantic
Treaty. (The original 12 were joined in 1951 by Greece and
Turkey, in 1955 by West Germany, and in 1982 by Spain.)
This treaty was notable for four articles:

▸ *Article 2:* A pledge to take practical steps to carry out
the lofty principles of the preamble with respect to

7

safeguarding "the freedom, common heritage and civilization of their peoples" by "strengthening their free institutions [and] by bringing about a better understanding of the principles upon which these institutions are founded," thus giving the Atlantic alliance a political rationale sadly lacking in many other instances.

▶ *Article 3:* An undertaking to "maintain and develop their individual and collective capacity to resist armed attack."

▶ *Article 4:* An agreement to consult together whenever "the territorial integrity, political independence or security of any of the Parties is threatened."

▶ *Article 5:* A commitment by each signatory to regard an armed attack against one or more of them (within certain geographic areas) as an attack against them all and, consequently, to take "such action as it deems necessary, including the use of armed force, to restore and maintain the security of the North Atlantic area."

This last provision was crucial, since it invoked the classic rationale of any treaty of alliance: to multiply the strength of its members beyond anything they were capable of mustering individually. This was particularly true of the Atlantic alliance, since it brought in the United States, whose economic strength and military capacity were essential if NATO was to succeed in providing a political and military counterbalance to the power of the Soviet Union. Equally, the alliance bound together most of the countries of Western Europe in peaceful and productive relationships which could put an end to the cycle of wars that had devastated Europe in the twentieth century. Moreover, it ensured that the weight and influence of the United States would be devoted to this task as well as to that of deterring any Soviet incursion or resisting any Soviet pressure. It is easy, therefore, to see what the European members gained from the Atlantic alliance.

8

What, however, motivated the United States to join what political analyst Robert Osgood quite aptly called the entangling alliance? Among the reasons was that of preventing any European power from gaining hegemony over the region, a goal for which America had twice gone to war in a single generation. Another was a belief that without some moves to check Soviet expansionism, i.e., to "contain" the U.S.S.R., there was no hope of altering its behavior and persuading it to play a more constructive role in the world community. A third was a sense of shared values, which made it easier and more necessary to join with the countries of Europe in forming an alliance than with those of other regions. In the words of Manfred Wörner, subsequently NATO secretary-general, the Atlantic alliance "became the expression of a common purpose and a political vision, a community of values and destiny...to ensure the cohesion and solidarity of our liberal democracies." And there was, of course, another reason: through the alliance, the United States gained support for measures it would have taken anyway in its own interest.

Perhaps the decision to join NATO was easier than it might have been because none of the alliance's political leaders in 1949 anticipated an attack by the Soviet Union. Rather, they saw their task as that of restoring self-confidence by creating a modest military shield behind which the West would proceed with economic reconstruction and, in the words of U.S. elder statesman George F. Kennan, the creation of "a new ordering of international relations...so patently worthy and inspiring in itself, and so wholly without menace to anyone anywhere, that peoples could safely repair to it without raising military issues."

Two events, however, shattered that belief in the efficacy of "a modest military shield." One was the detonation by the U.S.S.R. in September 1949 of its first atomic bomb, which ended the U.S. monopoly of nuclear weapons, and the other was the invasion of South Korea by North Korea in June 1950, an event which was taken (erroneously, it would appear) as a sign that the Soviet Union would not hesitate to use force to achieve its ends.

The Development of NATO during the Cold War

Even before the Korean War (1950–53), the members of NATO had begun to build a civilian and military framework for decisionmaking, to devise a strategic concept for the integrated defense of the North Atlantic area, to determine the forces required to implement that concept and to develop a program for the production and supply of arms and equipment. All these efforts moved into high gear after June 1950, when it seemed possible that the Soviets might attack Western Europe.

Since such a concept had to take account of the different geostrategic positions and differing perspectives of Europeans and North Americans, to reflect and incorporate the ever-changing nuclear technology, to be acceptable politically and to be bearable financially, it proved hard to devise. After abandoning, in turn, a conventional defense strategy (which was too costly and too vulnerable to nuclear weapons) and one relying on "massive retaliation" (which became questionable when the U.S.S.R. developed the capacity to deliver nuclear missiles on U.S. targets), NATO in 1967 endorsed the concept of "flexible response." This strategy called for a conventional defense against a conventional attack where this seemed feasible, for deliberate escalation to the selective use of nuclear weapons when it did not, and/or for a general nuclear response, according to the nature and magnitude of the threat. This formula was sufficiently ambiguous, especially about the circumstances in which escalation would take place, to be acceptable both to the Europeans and the Americans. Europeans, generally speaking, viewed nuclear weapons as an offset to their weakness in conventional forces, and Americans wished to strengthen these forces so that NATO could avoid having to use nuclear weapons, except in response to a Soviet strike. And though disputes over the concept and the resources required to implement flexible response flared up from time to time, it remained in effect until after the end of the cold war. (Interestingly enough, neither Americans nor Europeans paid much attention to *Soviet* military doctrine, which called for utilizing nuclear weapons from the beginning of any war—and perhaps even using them first, if war seemed imminent. Hence, Soviet analysts tended to view the debates within the alliance as both esoteric and irrelevant.) Since the defense of Europe required an effective military establishment, NATO set out to acquire one. Its leaders pushed and prodded the member states into improving the readiness of their armed forces for combat, into coordinating the planning for their use in time of war and into earmarking them for employment by the Integrated Military Command Structure. To back up its troops, NATO built installations and facilities such as airfields, communications and information systems, military headquarters, fuel pipelines and storage tanks, radar and navigational aids, etc., which could be used by multinational forces. It attempted to promote standardization of equipment, to engage in joint procurement planning and to enter into the cooperative production of items such as aircraft and ground-to-air missiles. And it tried to coordinate both the logistic planning and the armaments production of the member nations. Despite limited success in the latter two areas, NATO did manage to create powerful forces, nuclear and conventional.

These solid achievements in the military field were not matched in the other areas. For one thing, not every member of the Atlantic alliance adhered to "the principles of democracy, individual liberty and the rule of law." Portugal, Greece and Turkey all, at various times, had authoritarian governments. For another, Greece and Turkey violated Article 1 of the North Atlantic Treaty, which called for settling disputes peacefully and for refraining from the threat or use of force. As for "encouraging" economic cooperation, except for consulting on developments with a direct bearing on security, NATO let other institutions, such as the Organization for Economic Cooperation and Development (OECD), which began operations in 1961, handle such matters. And NATO's Public Information Program, for understandable reasons, concentrated on enhancing awareness of the role and achievements of the alliance, leaving to others the task of "bringing about a better understanding of the principles upon which these [free] institutions are founded." Thus, despite the importance attached by the signatories to political and economic factors, NATO paid most attention to issues and programs with a direct bearing on security.

In Pursuit of Détente

Among these were two areas with political overtones. One was the promotion of better relations with the Soviet Union and the countries of Eastern Europe, a recommendation made in the Report on the Future Tasks of the Alliance, produced by a committee under the chairmanship of the Belgian foreign minister, Pierre Harmel. Given that the alternatives were war or an unending period of hostility and tension, a policy of détente *and* collective defense (which is what the Harmel Report endorsed) must have seemed sensible. In any event, the allies embarked on a long series of meetings and negotiations with their adversaries. Some undertakings, like the 1969 *Ostpolitik* of West German Chancellor Willy Brandt (which emphasized contacts and some forms of cooperation with the Soviet Union), were bilateral; others, like the Conference on Security and Cooperation in Europe, which opened in Helsinki, Finland, in 1973, were multilateral. Though the process encountered many obstacles, not least those resulting from changes in Soviet—and American—leadership, it did help bring about an improvement in relations with the Soviet Union and Eastern Europe. And this paved the way for the more rapid and far-reaching relaxation of tensions that occurred when Mikhail S. Gorbachev became general secretary of the Communist party of the Soviet Union in 1985 and contributed significantly to ending the cold war.

Along with political détente went "military détente," or efforts to control and limit arms, to which the Harmel Report paid special attention. For a long time, progress in this area was virtually nonexistent. For instance, the negotiations on mutual and balanced force reductions (MBFR) dragged on for years, largely because NATO was seeking cutbacks in Warsaw Pact forces in Europe which the Soviet Union and the other pact members deemed unacceptable. (The Warsaw Treaty Organization, also known as the Warsaw Pact, consisted of the Soviet Union, plus Albania, Bulgaria, Czechoslovakia, German Democratic Republic, Hungary, Poland and Romania. It was formed in 1955 as a counterpoise to NATO. Although structured very differently, it carried out the same functions of assessing threats, devising responses and developing the forces required to implement them as its Western counterpart.) Although there had been some minor agreements, such as the establishment in 1963 of a "hot line" between Moscow and Washington for use in time of crisis and the limitation on testing nuclear weapons, the first measure actually to control weapons did not occur until 1972, with the signature of a strategic arms limitation agreement (SALT I), which put some curbs on the development of strategic nuclear delivery vehicles, and a subsequent expansion of these curbs under SALT II in 1977. The first arms control agreement to affect Europe directly was the INF treaty signed in Washington in December 1987, which eliminated all U.S. and Soviet land-based intermediate-range nuclear forces (including the hundreds deployed in Europe). And though an agreement to reduce conventional forces in Europe (CFE) was not reached until 1990, and that eliminating short-range missiles, rockets and nuclear-capable artillery until still later, by the beginning of 1989 changes in the military balance in Europe were already under way.

So, too, were changes in NATO thinking. Although the Europeans still relied on the U.S. nuclear guarantee for their security, they no longer insisted that prompt, large-scale retaliation was essential to deterrence. Indeed, the debate focused on the size and nature of the initial response, which was intended to remind the Soviets of the risk of continuing an attack rather than to destroy the U.S.S.R., in whole or in part. Moreover, some allies had come to believe that the danger of having ground-based nuclear weapons systems on European soil outweighed their potential contribution to deterrence, and hence were willing to remove them. And conventional forces, while

NATO's Civil and Military Structure

National Authorities

Permanent Representatives
(Ambassadors to NATO)

Military
Representatives
to NATO

Defense Planning Committee

North Atlantic Council

Nuclear Planning Group

Military Committee

SECRETARY GENERAL

Major NATO Commands

Allied Command Europe

Allied Command Atlantic

Canada-U.S. Regional Planning Group

OTHER COMMITTEES
Areas of Responsibility

- Political Affairs
- Political-Military Affairs
- Partnership and Cooperation
- Verification Coordination
- Economics
- Information
- Force Planning
- Nuclear Planning
- Resource Planning
- Budgets
- Infrastructure
- Armaments Cooperation
- Standardization
- Defense Research
- Communications and Information Systems
- Air Defense
- Logistic Support
- Civil Emergency Planning
- European Air Space Coordination
- Council Operations and Exercises
- Scientific Affairs
- Environmental Issues
- Security

Source: *NATO Handbook, 1995*

still deficient in modern equipment, supplies of ammunition and trained reserves, were deemed by all except the Americans (who clung to the belief that NATO should be prepared to conduct a prolonged conventional defense) to be reasonably adequate for the limited role they would play in the event of war. These alterations in judgments did not stem so much from shifts in the military balance (which, despite the rearmament program of the Reagan Administration, 1981–89, remained relatively stable) as they did from changes in the political atmosphere. Détente and arms control, which key figures in the Reagan Administration had viewed with skepticism, had by 1989 gained grudging acceptance in the United States and enthusiastic endorsement in the Soviet Union, so the stage was set for further measures to reduce the fear of war and the burden of armaments. This, however, is another story, and before telling it, it will be useful to examine the process by which NATO reaches decisions on such weighty matters.

How Does NATO Work?

Devising and putting into effect all these policies and programs required not only strong political leadership but experienced and knowledgeable advisers and a capable staff. Moreover, these individuals could not have operated over a period of 40 years and on so vast a scale without an organizational structure. Hence, one of the first things NATO did was to establish such a structure, the North Atlantic Treaty Organization.

Over the years, NATO grew to include (see chart):

▸ The North Atlantic Council (NAC), which, together with its ancillary bodies, the Defense Planning Committee and the Nuclear Planning Group, has effective political authority and power of decision. The council, comprising representatives of all member countries, meets at the level of ambassadors at least once a week and it also meets several times a year at higher levels involving the foreign ministers or the heads of state and government.

NATO's Integrated Military Command Structure

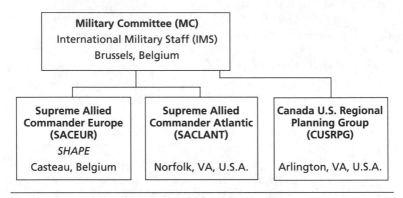

Military Committee (MC) International Military Staff (IMS) Brussels, Belgium		
Supreme Allied Commander Europe (SACEUR) *SHAPE* Casteau, Belgium	**Supreme Allied Commander Atlantic (SACLANT)** Norfolk, VA, U.S.A.	**Canada U.S. Regional Planning Group (CUSRPG)** Arlington, VA, U.S.A.

▶ The secretary-general of NATO, who is nominated by member nations, serves *ex officio* as chairman of the North Atlantic Council, the Defense Planning Committee, the Nuclear Planning Group and other senior committees. He (or she) also acts as principal spokesman of the alliance and is responsible for the work of the international staff, which serves the council and the committees and working groups subordinate to it.

▶ The Military Committee, which consists of the chief of staff of each member country except France and Iceland (which has no armed forces), or their representatives. The Military Committee is responsible for recommending to NATO's political authorities those measures considered necessary for the common defense of the NATO area and for providing guidance on military matters to the major NATO commanders. The committee is supported by an International Military Staff, which works in a number of specialized areas such as intelligence, plans and policy, operations and logistics.

What makes NATO so effective militarily is the Integrated Military Command Structure (see chart above). This structure consists of the Military Committee, the International Military Staff, the Canada/U.S. Regional Planning Group, two major commands, that of the Supreme Allied Commander Europe (Saceur) and that of the Supreme Allied Commander Atlantic (Saclant), and a number of subordinate military commands. The major commands are responsible for the development of defense plans for their respective areas, for the determination of force requirements, for the deployment and training of forces under their command or control and, in time of war, for the conduct of military operations. (Contrary to popular belief, these commanders do not normally have troops under their control in peacetime, except for small elements intended for use in a crisis.)

What is as important as what NATO tries to do is how it tries to do it, and here it is driven by the fact that it is not a supranational organization but a multinational one. (As the *NATO Handbook* phrases it, "It is an intergovernmental organization in which member countries retain their sovereignty and independence.") This means that the representatives must endeavor simultaneously to forward their nation's interests, reconcile them with those of other member states and further the objectives of NATO. In this process of determining the "collective will," each member has equal voice. There is no voting or decision by majority, and action is based on unanimity and common accord. This process apparently applies not only at the top but in the various lower-level committees and working groups.

The success or failure of this approach depends in large measure on the interactions among the national delegations of the member states, the international staff and the governments of the participating countries. In military matters, for example, governments, which retain full freedom of action, determine the size and nature of their armed forces and the elements, if any, they will earmark for collective defense. They are, of course, supposed to take into account the overall needs of the alliance, and the NATO defense plan provides methods and machinery for doing this. The first step is for NATO headquarters to prepare the strategic guidance, which indicates how NATO would conduct operations if forced to do so. The second step is for the major commanders, Saceur and Saclant, to determine how they would implement that guidance and to estimate the forces they would need. Their plans and requirements are reviewed (and adjusted) by the Military Committee and passed on to the Defense Planning Committee for its approval. It is then up to the staff of NATO and the national delegations to persuade the member governments to support NATO force goals set by the Defense Planning Committee.

There are, understandably, limits to the impact that NATO can have. Every nation (not least the United States) has insisted on maintaining its own armed forces, which are organized, trained and equipped to serve national ends as well as those of the Atlantic alliance. Moreover, many member nations, concerned both about jobs and about the maintenance of defense industries, have insisted on producing much of their own equipment, even at the expense of standardization and the ability to operate together. Furthermore, logistics, including transportation, remains a national responsibility. Hence, American troops moving to Europe do so in U.S. ships and aircraft, use U.S. weapons and equipment already stockpiled in Europe or brought from the United States, draw on American depots for supplies, and, if sick or wounded, are cared for in American military hospitals. In case the point needs underscoring, NATO is an alliance of sovereign nations, not a supranational organization, and this affects both the efficiency and the effectiveness of NATO defenses.

Does NATO Work?

NATO has developed over time into a complex, specialized organization designed to deal with everything from the threat of war in southeastern Europe to the choices between competing communications systems. But its very complexity works against it, as does the fact that it is multinational. (French emperor Napoleon said that one reason for his success was that most of his wars were fought against allies.) Whatever the desirability of, indeed the political necessity for, decisionmaking based on consensus among 16 members, it is a cumbersome process. One reason is the difficulty of getting 16 people to agree on anything! A second is that the member states may have interests which they seek to pursue through NATO, in competition with, and sometimes in contention with, other members following their particular interests. And a third is that, even if they put NATO interests ahead of those of their respective homelands, representatives may differ as to the course that NATO should take. This was true during the disputes over nuclear strategy in the 1960s and 1970s.

The display of unanimity in NATO communiqués belies the fact that the members of NATO are rarely of one mind. Indeed, they are not always of one view concerning the utility of NATO as the "essential forum for consultation among its members and the venue for agreement on policies bearing on the security and defense commitments of the allies...", to quote a phrase found commonly in NATO communiqués. At various times virtually every member state has bypassed NATO in favor of bilateral negotiations with other powers or unilateral action. U.S. President Ronald Reagan met privately with Gorbachev at Reykjavik, Iceland, in 1986 to discuss the abolition of nuclear weapons. When Turkey dispatched troops to Cyprus in 1974, it acted unilaterally. These and other instances are reminders that NATO is not the vehicle for all Allied activities, even when they impinge upon the "stability and wellbeing" of the North Atlantic area.

Under these circumstances it is surprising that NATO has worked at all. In fact there have been flaming rows (as over U.S. aid to Israel during the October 1973 war) and long periods when a consensus could not be reached (as over what military action to take in Bosnia). On the whole, however, NATO has managed to present a unified front on issues ranging from German unification to changes in nuclear arsenals.

One reason for this has been the realization by all members that NATO is indispensable to European security and that too much foot-dragging or too much opposition to particular measures might weaken it, to their detriment. Another is that the members have developed ways of dealing with issues outside the formal process, sometimes through the intercession of one or more representatives with a hesitant colleague, at other times using appeals at the governmental level, and from time to time by playing political hardball. (According to former Secretary of State Henry A. Kissinger, when some of the Europeans balked at U.S. proposals for coping with the Arab oil embargo of 1973, President Richard M. Nixon "issued a veiled threat to pull U.S. troops out of Europe unless the NATO allies abandoned their intransigence on oil.") A third reason was that during the cold war, when American military support was essential, the United States exercised a frequently decisive influence. Whatever the theoretical basis for the claim that the voice of the foreign minister of Luxembourg echoed as loudly as that of the U.S. secretary of state, it was palpable nonsense—and both of these gentlemen knew it. And finally, though doubt as to whether the Soviet Union *would* employ force had been growing for years, the fact that it had the capability to do so meant that the allies had to—and did—focus on measures to preclude this. Whether this enforced unity will survive the end of the cold war is another question.

2

Developments Since 1989 and NATO's Response

THE NATO described in the preceding chapter was devised for the Europe of 1989, when not only Germany itself but most of Europe was divided into competing blocs, marked by different political systems and ideologies and pursuing very different interests, in Europe and outside of it. Even more importantly, each bloc feared the use of force by the other and so developed and deployed both powerful nuclear arsenals and massive armies, navies and air forces. Since then, the environment in which NATO must operate has changed drastically. What are those changes, and how has NATO reacted to them?

Since 1989, Germany has been united and Soviet control over the countries of Eastern Europe lifted, leaving them free to create their own political institutions and pursue their own paths toward economic development. Moreover, the Soviet Union itself has dissolved into its constituent republics, some of which joined together in 1991 in a weak Commonwealth of Independent States (CIS) and others of which became completely independent. These changed circumstances put a final end to the confrontation between East and West; made possible large-scale interactions, political, economic and cultural, between the countries of Europe and parts of the CIS; facilitated progress on the establishment of human rights and the rule of law; and enabled reasonable people to dream of a "new Europe," with peace, prosperity and security for all.

Militarily, the changes were even more dramatic. For one, Soviet/Russian troops have been withdrawn from Eastern Europe, partly disarmed under the provisions of the conventional forces in Europe treaty, drastically reduced in size and thoroughly demoralized by the political, economic and social changes that have taken place in their homeland. Moreover, the Warsaw Treaty Organization has been dissolved and the armed forces of the former East European members reduced in size, reorganized and reoriented. For example, the army of the Czech Republic is being restructured so that it will both resemble and be compatible with the armed forces of Western Europe, with which it is preparing to cooperate in peacekeeping operations and with whom it hopes to be integrated through NATO. The missiles that were part of the theater nuclear forces (TNF) on both sides have been scrapped and the airborne carriers reduced in number. Moreover, the strategic nuclear forces (SNF) of the United States and Russia have also been reduced, with more cuts planned for the end of the century.

This does not mean that the millennium has arrived, but it does suggest that the danger of a massive onslaught from the East, backed up by threats to employ nuclear weapons if necessary, no longer exists. While there is a possibility that a "resurgent Russia" may again muster the strength and the determination to pursue aggressive policies in Europe, this is very remote. Instead, the threats to European security derive from

▶ political instability, stemming from the economic dislocation attendant on the collapse of communism and the difficulties of introducing new political systems, with Russia as perhaps the prime example.

22

- ethnic conflicts, the product of long-suppressed national rivalries exacerbated by the crazy-quilt pattern of ethnic settlements in Europe, which do not conform to state boundaries, most notably in Eastern Europe and in the territories of the former Soviet Union.

- threats arising outside of Europe, ranging from an attack by nuclear-armed terrorists to interference with the flow of oil.

In consequence, the concern of West Europeans is not about deliberate aggression but about becoming involved in civil wars or interstate conflicts, not about an avalanche of tanks but about a flood of refugees, not about defending their own territories from attack but about undertaking peacekeeping or peacemaking missions elsewhere. And these changes have impacted directly on NATO, whose members must consider not only how they will cope with this new military situation but whether NATO is the most appropriate instrument. In so doing, they must consider changes in the "security architecture of Europe" as other organizations start to develop—the Organization for (formerly the Conference on) Security and Cooperation in Europe (OSCE), the European Union and the Western European Union.

Organization for Security and Cooperation in Europe

The OSCE is a body encompassing all the countries of Europe and all the republics of the former Soviet Union, plus Canada and the United States: 55, if one counts Yugoslavia (which is suspended) and the Former Yugoslav Republic of Macedonia (FYRM), an observer. (For membership in this and other organizations, see "A Growing Network of Institutions," page 32.) The OSCE establishes standards of conduct for member states, provides a permanent forum for dialogue on matters relating to security in Europe and is the main instrument for developing confidence-building measures and for promoting arms control in Europe. While the OSCE is too large, too diverse and too weak militarily to be a guarantor of security in the traditional meaning of that word, it does try to head off burgeoning conflicts, whether interstate or intrastate; to endeavor to negotiate cease-fires and, if possible, political settlements; and otherwise to inhibit local conflicts from spreading or festering. Moreover, the OSCE can, as part of the process of conflict resolution, authorize peacekeeping operations (to be carried out by the OSCE itself or subcontracted to particular states or groups of states, such as NATO). Thus, the OSCE plays a major role in the political-diplomatic aspects of security.

European Union

Another important organization, with a different purpose, is the European Union (EU), in existence since 1993. The EU evolved from the European Coal and Steel Community (ECSC, 1952), the European Atomic Energy Community (Euratom, 1958) and the European Economic Community (EEC, 1958). As its name indicates, the European Union is seeking to integrate more fully the activities of its member states and to become the nexus of a new Europe. At the moment it consists of 15 states from Northern, Western and Southern Europe, but it may soon include some of the countries of Eastern Europe. Unlike the OSCE, the EU does not focus solely on security; in fact, its aim is to integrate the economic systems and financial structures of its members, to harmonize their social policies and to coordinate their political activities. The EU is, however, also endeavoring to formulate a common foreign and security policy, which could involve it in issues ranging from checking nuclear proliferation to coping with the consequences of conflicts; in fact, it has been heavily engaged in administering and rebuilding the town of Mostar, in Bosnia, as part of the 1995 Dayton peace accord. More importantly, it has determined that the common foreign and security policy shall "include all questions related to the security of the EU, including the eventual framing of a common defense policy, which might in time lead to a common defense." And it has asked the WEU to "elaborate and implement decisions and actions of the council [of the European Union] which have defense implications."

Western European Union

The WEU is, like NATO, a collective defense organization comprising, in one category or another, all nations belonging to the EU, the European members of NATO and nine countries from Eastern Europe, a total of 27. Although only the 10 full members are bound to aid each other by force of arms, others have agreed to consider employing their military units for "humanitarian and rescue tasks; for peacekeeping tasks; and for tasks of combat forces in crisis management, including peacemaking"—missions which NATO is also preparing to undertake.

Moreover, the WEU is also tasked with becoming the "European pillar of the Atlantic alliance," a role with even greater potential for interactions with NATO. Whether the WEU eventually takes over some of the tasks currently performed by NATO, up to and including the defense of European members against external aggression, or serves primarily to coordinate and enhance the European contribution to NATO's work, or does both, it certainly must be taken into account in considering the future of NATO.

The Response by NATO

NATO had to respond to the new situation after the cold war or run the risk of becoming irrelevant. Thus, NATO embarked in 1991 on a series of measures intended to enable it to play a major role in shaping the future of Europe. As a first step, NATO reevaluated the threats to the security of the treaty area, which now include, in addition to possible attacks on member states:

(1) "Instabilities...ethnic rivalries and territorial disputes... in Central and Eastern Europe";

(2) "Risks of a wider nature, including...disruption of the flow of vital resources [such as oil]..."; and

25

(3) "Proliferation of weapons of mass destruction,...and actions of terrorism and sabotage."

Next, it revised its strategy to deal with these potential threats, emphasizing "power projection" outside the NATO area rather than defense of a line across the center of Europe. It also readjusted its force postures to provide the more mobile and flexible forces needed to carry out this mission. Even more importantly, it authorized the establishment of Combined Joint Task Forces, with commanders and staffs from the major military commands and ground, air and/or naval forces from within and without NATO. These are to be activated in time of emergency and used for NATO missions other than collective defense (such as that in Bosnia) and/or for operations in which only some members wish to take part. And finally, NATO has begun to revise its Integrated Military Command Structure and its planning structure to facilitate decisions on, and the conduct of, the very different kinds of operations envisioned under the new strategy. Thus, NATO has undertaken (though it has not yet completed) far-reaching changes in its military arm.

Equally extensive changes have been made in the political dimension of NATO. As a political counterpart to this military realignment, NATO has taken special responsibility for crisis prevention and crisis management, including consideration of requests for peacekeeping forces made by the Organization for Security and Cooperation in Europe and/or the United Nations. (In fact, the initial NATO involvement in Yugoslavia, in the form of naval blockades, air patrols and air strikes, was a direct result of a request by the UN to provide support for humanitarian operations in Bosnia, and the current one, in support of the Dayton peace accord, stemmed from a recognition by all parties that no other organization could do the job.)

Partnership for Peace

Both as a military measure and because it served broader purposes (such as promoting democracy and ending the division of Europe between East and West) NATO also established

**President Clinton discussed NATO expansion and Russia's
place in a new Europe with Russian President Yeltsin in
Helsinki, Finland, in March 1997.**

the Partnership for Peace (PFP) in 1994. Partners, who include
the United States, Canada, most of the states of Europe, plus a
number of the Asian republics of the Commonwealth of Independent States, commit themselves to refrain from the threat
or use of force, to preserving democratic societies and to making more open their national defense planning. They also identify the facilities, resources and forces they are willing to make
available to the partnership and the extent to which they are
prepared to participate in joint planning, training and operations. NATO works out with each partner a program of training
and exercises in areas such as rescue operations, disaster relief,
peacekeeping and crisis management, and it invites each partner to send representatives to NATO headquarters and to a
Partnership Coordination Cell, which is responsible for the
military planning necessary to implement the partnership programs. Perhaps more importantly, NATO pledges to consult
with any participant if that partner perceives a direct threat to
its security.

North Atlantic Cooperation Council

The partnership is part of a larger effort to enhance the security of nonmembers of NATO and to promote stable democratic governments in the states of the former Communist bloc. Another instrument is the North Atlantic Cooperation Council (NACC), which brings together the members of NATO, the erstwhile republics of the U.S.S.R., the East European states formerly belonging to the Warsaw Pact and a number of other countries in Europe. As the acronym suggests, NACC (pronounced nack-see) was formed to promote cooperation among former adversaries through consultations on political and security-related matters, by exchanges of views on military affairs such as defense planning, key aspects of strategy and command structures, and by means of practical measures to improve defense planning and budgeting, civilian control of the military, procurement of equipment for the armed forces, etc. Moreover, NACC has been heavily involved in plans and preparations for peacekeeping operations, a task which it now shares with the PFP. (NACC and PFP do not differ very much; in fact, NATO is now considering merging some of their activities, especially with respect to peacekeeping.)

Other Activities

Both through NACC and bilaterally, NATO has endeavored to engage Russia in the task of promoting peace and stability in Europe. To this end, it has not only highlighted Russia's participation in the PFP but also held discussions on a charter which could spell out the areas in which NATO and Russia might cooperate, as well as the conditions governing their relationship. Moreover, NATO has involved Russia in the peacekeeping operations in Bosnia, while Britain, France, Germany and the United States have added Russia to the contact group, which has played a key role in setting policy with respect to Bosnia. Additionally, key member states have, on their own, sought to help Russia prepare to play a constructive role in the new Europe.

The last measure to enhance stability in Eastern Europe and promote democracy in the post-Communist states is much further reaching, going far beyond the partnership and the coordination council. The Atlantic alliance has proposed to offer membership in NATO to "democratic states to our east," *with a guarantee of assistance in the event of attack.* While all the states of the Organization for Security and Cooperation in Europe were invited to join the PFP, the list for admission to NATO is much more restricted: invitees must not only be in a position to "further the principles of the treaty" (which include democracy, individual liberty and the rule of law) but also "to contribute to the security of the North Atlantic area." Thus, more is asked of them, and more is given.

In addition, NATO has nurtured relations with other institutions closely concerned with European security, the OSCE and the Western European Union as well as the UN. NATO's collaboration with the UN grew out of its willingness to support UN peacekeeping initiatives in Yugoslavia. It has included joint conferences on the theory and practice of peacekeeping, general discussions on the role NATO could play, visits by high-level officials to the two headquarters and even consideration of establishing a NATO liaison mission at the UN.

Interactions with the OSCE focused on helping that organization extend the scope of its activities beyond dialogue and the setting of values, strengthening its internal mechanisms and decisionmaking processes, as well as supporting efforts to enhance its capabilities for early warning, conflict prevention and crisis management. NATO offered to consider supporting OSCE peacekeeping operations and suggested a "rational allocation of tasks and missions to various organizations," something which has still to be worked out.

NATO has paid the greatest attention to relations with the WEU, which it has accepted as the "defense component of the European Union." It has pledged to support the development of the European Security and Defense Identity (ESDI) within NATO and has taken a number of practical steps to do so, including the identification of "separable but not separate" military capabilities that could be used by WEU, and the planning and conduct of training exercises for illustrative WEU missions. Whether these will suffice to build a European defense component depends what position WEU will hold in the "security architecture of Europe," a question which has not yet been resolved.

Unfinished Business

Although NATO has changed significantly since 1989, it has still to complete its adaptation to the new Europe. In some instances, this is because the weight of the past militates against rapid alterations in the way it does things. This is particularly true with regard to the Integrated Military Command Structure, where readjustments must take account of multiple military missions with differing requirements, of varying national positions and of the not infrequent clash between what leaders deem politically desirable and what commanders deem militarily necessary—as epitomized by the dispute over ultimate command responsibility in Combined Joint Task Forces.

In other cases, the slowness of response stems not so much from the influence of the past as it does from differences over how to translate principle into practice. The disagreements stem from divergent national interests, conflicting assessments of the situation and varying concepts of the role that NATO should play. Although these factors influence decisions on virtually every matter coming before NATO, there are four issues of such importance that they warrant special consideration: (1) *The extension of the treaty area through the admission of new members.* This could change both the nature of NATO and the steps it may have to take to maintain peace and security in Europe; (2) *Relations with Russia.* Russia's cooperation with the West is essential to the creation of a new Europe, but its past practices and current policies arouse suspicions in the minds of many; (3) *NATO's place in the "architecture of Europe."* Among the unresolved questions are the long-term relations between NATO, WEU and the EU; (4) *The conduct of peacekeeping operations.* Though NATO has agreed to undertake these, their implementation is fraught with difficulty, as events in Bosnia have shown.

3

NATO and Its Partners

NATO DECLARED in January 1994 that it "expect[s] and would welcome NATO expansion that would reach to democratic states to our east…" This process is now under way. Although the reasons for this offer ranged from a desire to end the division of Europe to a belief that the West should seal the "victory" won in the cold war, two sets of arguments seemingly were decisive. Many leaders from the Baltic republics and the nations of Eastern Europe asserted that admission to NATO would enhance their sense of security, give them political backing and military support against possible aggression and open up new avenues for interactions with the West, thereby enabling them to develop along lines of their own choosing. Germany and other members of the alliance argued that enlargement, by helping maintain in Eastern Europe stable democracies closely tied to the West, would strengthen security in the region for all states, members and nonmembers. Moreover, they saw expansion as part of NATO's dynamic response to a changing Europe, where the security challenges and risks are very different from those of the past.

Not all members of the Atlantic alliance held this view. Some

A Growing Network of Institutions

CSCE: Conference on Security and Cooperation in Europe (1973; Known as Organization for Security and Cooperation in Europe (OSCE) since December 1994.)
NACC: North Atlantic Cooperation Council (1991)
PFP: Partnership for Peace (1994; NATO members and states that signed a PFP Framework Agreement but not necessarily an Individual Partnership Program.)
NATO: North Atlantic Treaty Organization (1949)
EU: European Union, formerly the European Community (1957)
WEU: West European Union (1954)
CIS: Commonwealth of Independent States (1991)

	CSCE	NACC	PFP	NATO	EU	WEU	CIS
United States	■	■	■	■			
Canada	■	■	■	■			
Belgium	■	■	■	■	■	■	
France	■	■	■	■	■	■	
Germany	■	■	■	■	■	■	
Italy	■	■	■	■	■	■	
Luxembourg	■	■	■	■	■	■	
Netherlands	■	■	■	■	■	■	
Portugal	■	■	■	■	■	■	
Spain	■	■	■	■	■	■	
United Kingdom	■	■	■	■	■	■	
Greece	■	■	■	■	■	■	
Denmark	■	■	■	■	■	■	◆
Iceland	■	■	■	■		●	
Norway	■	■	■	■		●	
Turkey	■	■	■	■		●	
Ireland	■				■	◆	
Austria	■	◆	■		■	◆	
Finland	■	◆	■		■	◆	
Sweden	■	◆	■		■	◆	
Switzerland	■		■				
Czech Republic	■	■	■		3	▲	
Hungary	■	■	■		3	▲	
Poland	■	■	■		3	▲	
Slovakia	■	■	■		3	▲	

	CSCE	NACC	PFP	NATO	EU	WEU	CIS
Bulgaria	■	■	■		3	▲	
Romania	■	■	■		3	▲	
Albania	■	■	■				
Estonia	■	■	■		3	▲	
Latvia	■	■	■		3	▲	
Lithuania	■	■	■		3	▲	
Russia	■	■	■		4		■
Ukraine	■	■	■		4		■
Moldova	■	■	■		4		■
Azerbaijan	■	■	■		4		■
Georgia	■	■	■		4		■
Kazakstan	■	■	■		4		■
Turkmenistan	■	■	■				■
Armenia	■	■	■		4		■
Belarus	■	■	■		4		■
Kyrgyzstan	■	■	■		4		■
Tajikistan	■	■					■
Uzbekistan	■	■	■		4		■
Bosnia-Herzegovina	■						
Croatia	■						
F.Y.R. Macedonia	■	■					
Slovenia	■	■	■		3	▲	
Yugoslavia	2						
Others[1]	■	◆	■				

[1] Includes one or more of the following: Cyprus, the Holy See, Liechtenstein, Malta, Monaco and San Marino.
[2] "Yugoslavia" has been suspended.
[3] Signed "Europe agreement."
[4] Signed "partnership and cooperation agreement."

Sources: *The Military Balance 1996–97* (Oxford University Press for IISS); RAPID database of the EU; Facts on File weekly world news digest.

saw enlargement as irrelevant to the problems facing the states of Eastern Europe, and others as positively harmful because the emphasis on military matters would require the struggling economies to divert resources to the armed forces. There was a strong sense that economic growth might in the long run be a more important contribution to stability in Eastern Europe than military strength, and that membership in the European Union would open up vastly wider prospects than membership in NATO. The difficulty was that meeting the requirements for entry into the EU could take many years. Partly because of this consideration, partly because of enthusiastic American (and German) support, NATO endorsed enlargement.

While the rationale for expanding NATO is evident, so too are the drawbacks. On the military side, NATO would be taking on new obligations to defend relatively weak countries against external threats. Meeting such obligations could be difficult, not only because of the extent of territory to be defended but because some of the applicants for membership are, like the Baltic republics, geographically isolated. Thus NATO has had to consider the possible need to move troops from west to east in time of crisis or to station troops in peacetime on the soil of new members. Depending on estimates of the threat and whether it is necessary to strengthen local forces, make preparations to move troops from Western Europe or redeploy forces to Eastern Europe, the cost to the members of NATO, old and new, could range from $17 billion to $82 billion over the next 10 years. And this says nothing about the technical problems of preparing the armed forces of the nations of Eastern Europe to cooperate with existing NATO units and to work with NATO's Integrated Military Command Structure.

Difficult as membership would be militarily, it would be even more difficult politically. For one thing, admitting these countries would require every current member of the Atlantic alliance to regard an attack upon one of them as an attack upon all and would commit each to take action according to its constitutional procedures, under Article 5 of the North Atlantic Treaty. Such an obligation (which in the U.S. case would extend to the nuclear guarantee) would require not only legislative approval but also public support, which so far is lacking in many countries of NATO. Moreover, if expansion were to take place, the ability of the North Atlantic Council to agree on measures would be noticeably diminished: while Bulgaria and Hungary might have more interest in what happens in Yugoslavia than the Netherlands or Belgium, they are unlikely to have nearly as much interest in safeguarding passage through the Red Sea. Thus extending NATO eastward (and southeastward) might well weaken it, if it did not cause a fissure in the organization.

For another thing, Russian leaders (and particularly the Russian military) would see the extension of NATO territory from the Oder and Neisse rivers to the Bug and the Dnieper rivers as a threat to their country. As one Russian journalist wrote, NATO is aiming to change the whole post-cold-war European security structure to Russia's disadvantage. Already, the balance in conventional weapons had, with the signature of the conventional forces in Europe treaty and the dissolution of the Warsaw Treaty Organization, shifted in favor of NATO. Moreover, Russia can no longer count on the resources of the former states of the Soviet Union: some of them, like Ukraine, are resistant to measures to strengthen the Commonwealth of Independent States militarily, and others, like the Asian republics, are completely uninterested. The shift of the belt of "neutral states" in Eastern Europe to the NATO orbit can only be seen as another weakening of Russia's position, compounding the psychological shocks attendant on the disruption of the Soviet empire in Europe. Indeed, enlargement could once more bring NATO face-to-face with Russia, and it could strengthen the political elements opposing cooperation with the West.

Last, but by no means least, is the question of what to do with states not admitted to NATO. At the moment, alliance members seem to be split into three groups on the question of enlargement. One would limit it initially to a few countries deemed crucial for geostrategic reasons (Poland, the Czech Republic, Hungary and, should it meet the standards of democracy prescribed by NATO, perhaps Slovakia). Their admission would not overburden the alliance with new commitments and not seem so threatening to Russia. Another group (joined by leaders of some East European countries that are applicants for membership) would enlarge NATO in parallel with the expansion of the European Union, thereby giving a broader basis for European integration and providing a different rationale for admitting new members—that is, their ability to fit into a socioeconomic framework with the potential for becoming a political union. And a third group, spearheaded by the United States, would admit all who can meet the qualifications set by NATO, which in theory could include Ukraine and even Russia.

The difficulty is that all of these approaches would leave some states outside NATO, at least for the foreseeable future, and maybe for the long term. Not only would this redivide Europe but it could cause the disappointed applicants to lose confidence in the West and shirk the hard task of reshaping their political systems and economic structures along Western lines. These feelings would, of course, be exacerbated if one or more of the current members of NATO vetoed an applicant— a possibility that cannot be ruled out. Thus, NATO faces the task of providing a sense of security to new members at a level of costs and risks which current members will find acceptable, while simultaneously reassuring states not admitted to NATO of the organization's concern for their security and well-being.

Making New Members Feel More Secure

Broadly speaking, there are three ways of enhancing the sense of security of new members. One would be to emphasize the political benefits of joining NATO, whose new members will have all the rights and obligations of current ones. This means that they will participate fully in all the decisionmaking bodies and supporting staffs of NATO and, should they so choose, in the Integrated Military Command Structure, thereby linking themselves to the West. It means that they will be covered by Article 5 of the North Atlantic Treaty, shielded by the strategic nuclear forces of the alliance and protected by the conventional forces earmarked for collective defense. In this approach, NATO would try to make the new members feel that they are as much a part of the alliance as any other country— and as safe—without stationing troops, deploying nuclear weapons or establishing major military facilities on their soil. In fact, the model followed would be that of Norway.

Whether this will suffice to make the new members feel secure depends in some measure on their strategic positions and perceptions of threat. An additional step would be to provide further reassurance in the form of military installations and perhaps troop deployments on their territories, measures which are commonly regarded as surer guarantees of help in time of need than treaty provisions. Moreover, military planners, who have to consider how to back up political commitments, may also deem it desirable to prepare to do so by developing communications nets and logistic facilities, by stockpiling equipment and supplies, by reequipping local forces to enhance their consonance with other NATO elements, etc. The drawback is that an emphasis on collective defense may be costly. It may detract from efforts to cope with the crises and local conflicts that are the most likely threats to security, may frighten off potential endorsers of enlargement (who, like their political ancestors five decades earlier, may be more willing to pledge action when it does not seem necessary) and may seem to threaten neighboring states which, in the words of the *Study on NATO Enlargement*, may not join the alliance "either early or at all." Hence, a "full court press" may be unwise and (given the absence of a military threat to even an expanded NATO) unnecessary.

A third possibility might be to plan for collective defense only on a contingency basis and to relegate preparations for it to the time when the need for such measures is clear, a procedure which is now followed with regard to NATO's augmentation forces. Instead, emphasis might be placed initially on training and equipping local troops for the "new mission" of crisis management and peacekeeping operations, on building an infrastructure to support such operations and on conducting joint exercises at the lower end of the military spectrum, in this way maintaining a NATO presence without incurring the costs of preparations for large-scale military actions. Since NATO has indicated that it has "no a priori requirement for the stationing of alliance troops on the territory of new members," and it has explicitly declared that it has "no intention, no plan, and no reason" to deploy nuclear weapons there, such an approach might serve the NATO objectives of providing a sense of security to new members, being able to meet anticipated requirements for collective action and yet not seeming to threaten neighboring states, particularly Russia.

Linking Nonmembers to NATO

The second part of the task facing NATO is that of encouraging those states that do not join NATO "early or at all" to continue to play a significant role in promoting stability and security in an undivided Europe. NATO is already seeking to do this in three ways:

(1) Broadening the scope of the Partnership for Peace to include all of the alliance's new missions in crisis management. It is increasing the involvement of partners in NATO military planning, enhancing their participation in PFP activities and in political consultations, and it is offering them the opportunity to establish diplomatic missions with NATO.

(2) Proposing to establish an Atlantic Partnership Council, incorporating both the North Atlantic Cooperation Council and the Partnership for Peace, that would provide a framework for cooperation on practical matters and give an expanded political dimension to the partnership.

(3) Seeking, in these and other ways, to give concrete evidence of NATO's continuing support and concern for their security (including consultation in the event of a direct threat to a partner), to link them more closely with NATO, and to make the partnership part of the European security architecture.

These are all worthwhile measures in their own right and will go a long way toward blurring the distinction between new members of NATO and nonmembers. However, given the undoubted disappointment of applicants who are not accepted and the unease of states like Ukraine which do not feel they can even apply, further action might be considered. One possibility would be to negotiate special charters with states that do not become members, as NATO is currently doing with Ukraine, or draw up bilateral arrangements, as the United States is doing with the Baltic republics. Another possibility would be to help the Western European Union, in its role as the "European pillar" of NATO, to strengthen its interactions with aspirants to membership in NATO, virtually all of whom already are involved with the WEU, in one capacity or another. This would be particularly helpful in facilitating the "parallel enlargement" of NATO and the European Union, which is one objective of NATO. (Indeed, if NATO does, as it has hinted, "give particular consideration to countries with a perspective [sic] of EU membership and which have shown an interest in joining NATO," this could give such countries an additional incentive to pursue the economic reform, social progress and political adaptation that are the keys to entry into both organizations.)

There is, however, a further measure which may be the most important of all: defining more precisely the "new security architecture." NATO envisages this as being built through "a gradual process of integration and cooperation brought about by an interplay of existing multilateral institutions in Europe" and goes on to prescribe roles for these institutions. The role reserved for NATO is that of preserving peace in the Euro-Atlantic area and of providing security for its members. Yet not all the states of Europe will become members: some, like Switzerland, because they do not choose to do so; some, like Ukraine, because they dare not; and others, like Russia, because they cannot. How is *their* security to be ensured? How are they to be reassured that the "peace" that NATO maintains is in *their* interest and to *their* liking? It is both self-serving and incorrect to say that "enlargement will contribute to enhanced stability and security for all countries in the Euro-Atlantic area"; Russia, for one, does not think so. And as German Foreign Minister Klaus Kinkel pointed out, "Without bringing Russia into the system there will be no peace in Europe,…no new European architecture…."

4

Russia: Partner or
Threat to Security Again?

THE ISSUE OF NATO expansion illustrates perfectly the contradictions in NATO's views about and policy toward Russia. On the one hand, that country was invited to join the Partnership for Peace and to establish a special relationship with NATO, a move which is consistent with other efforts by the Western powers to persuade the Russian leaders that cooperation with the West pays dividends. On the other hand, concern that Russia might use its military power to enhance its influence over nearby states such as Poland and Lithuania was both a motivation for the decision to enlarge NATO and a reason for it to maintain a military capability for coping with a "resurgent Russia." What prompts NATO to take these divergent approaches?

The more conciliatory approach stems from NATO's recognition that this is both helpful to those elements in Russia that support cooperation with the West and the best way "to bring home the particular importance for European security of Russia seeing the alliance as a partner, not a threat." And, indeed, it has paid dividends in terms of progress in conventional and nuclear arms reductions, in the prevention of nuclear proliferation, in peacekeeping (with Russia's entry into the PFP and participation in the NATO-led Implementation Force in Bosnia as prime examples) and through membership in forums which seek to promote a common understanding of security problems and a consensus on how to deal with them.

The more cautious approach stems from concern that Russia's attempt to reintegrate the states belonging to the Commonwealth of Independent States into a "new" union might lead to the establishment of Russian hegemony and the creation of "a cohesive, coordinated military force under unified control and under Russia's nuclear protection...." Though Russia may well view such a development as a reasonable hedge against future extension of NATO to the east, its actualization may both increase pressures for such an extension and raise serious questions about NATO-Russian relations. This cautious approach derives also from concern that Russia's claim to the right to conduct peacekeeping operations on the territory of the former Soviet Union might lead to transgressions on the rights of other states and other peoples. Though Russia has sought approval of its operations from the UN Security Council and has endorsed the Organization for Security and Cooperation in Europe's efforts at mediation and conciliation in Georgia and Moldova, it has also employed peacekeeping forces to support one political faction against its rivals and one ethnic group against another.

This places NATO in a dilemma. Since it needs Russian acquiescence in peacekeeping measures which come before the OSCE and/or the UN Security Council, NATO is not likely to oppose the role Russia has claimed for itself in the "near abroad." NATO is even less likely to intervene in that area on its own. On the other hand, NATO could not remain passive in the face of what could become the reestablishment of Russian hegemony over the states formerly belonging to the U.S.S.R. Thus, the question is how NATO members can best influence Russia's attempt to secure a new "place in the sun."

The answer so far has been by a mix of admonition and conciliation. The former includes insisting that Russia work with the OSCE and the UN in peacekeeping operations, indicating strong support for countries such as Ukraine which feel pressured by Russia and pointing out the politically adverse consequences of, say, promoting Crimean "independence." The latter involves endeavoring to change Russian behavior rather than to criticize it too harshly (as in the case of Chechnya) and accepting negotiated outcomes to disputes between Russia and other states that are not wholly satisfactory to those states. This approach has produced some successes, as in the dampening of the conflict between the government of Moldova and the Russian minority in the so-called Republic of Trans-Dniester.

Russian Opposition

Not even this much can be claimed for efforts to persuade the Russians that the expansion of NATO would be in their interest. For one thing, many Russians do not accept the thesis that NATO is a "defense" alliance; they are concerned that enlargement would further tilt against them the balance in conventional forces; and they see the movement eastward of NATO troops as threatening to their security. For another, they view enlargement as a sign that the "victors" of the cold war are, to quote the former Russian general Aleksandr Lebed, "seeking a strategic advantage so they can deal with Russia from a position of strength." And, for a third, they see it as further diminishing their influence over developments in Europe, and the world at large. Thus, they have sought to block or to limit NATO expansion, to reduce the size and the capabilities of NATO forces on the soil of new members and to obtain a veto over the missions those forces could undertake.

For its part, NATO would find it difficult to slow down expansion, much less halt it, as Russia wishes, nor could it accept a Russian veto over the admission of particular countries, which might feel abandoned. Moreover, NATO cannot acquiesce in proposals that would enable Russia to block alliance decisions, such as the suggestion that the Organization for Security and Cooperation in Europe coordinate the security operations of all

European organizations, including not only NATO but the European Union, the Western European Union and the Commonwealth of Independent States. Nor can NATO agree to perpetual constraints on military measures aimed at enhancing the security of new members and/or preparing them to shoulder the burdens of membership. NATO, however, is concerned that enlargement may induce Russia to form a balancing coalition by reasserting control over some or all of the former Soviet neighbors; may dim the prospects for ratification of existing arms-control agreements, such as the Strategic Arms Reduction Treaty II, which was signed in 1993 but has not yet been approved by the Russian parliament; and may undermine the influence of democratizing elements in Russia. Accordingly, NATO—and the United States—have sought to temper the military effects of enlargement and to offset its political impact.

As one means to this end, NATO has indicated that it has no intention, now or in the foreseeable future, of permanently stationing foreign ground combat forces on the territories of new members, nor does it have any plans to introduce nuclear weapons onto their soil. Moreover, it has stated that the allies do not propose to install new weapons systems or establish new bases in Eastern Europe—as distinct from building communications nets, improving radar systems and otherwise seeking to enhance compatibility between the forces of old and new members. And it has proposed separately to renegotiate the conventional forces in Europe treaty so that the levels of equipment authorized for Western states are reduced and all weapons are counted on a national basis, rather than by blocs, measures which should ease Russian fears of a build-up of forces along its borders. Thus, NATO has sought to alleviate Russian concerns.

As part of this endeavor, NATO has offered Russia a charter which will provide for "consultation, cooperation and, to the maximum extent possible where appropriate, joint decision-making and action on security issues of common concern." Moreover, this charter will, at Russian insistence, codify some of the NATO pledges with regard to the stationing of forces and the deployment of weapons on the territories of new members and will provide for an increased Russian role in peace-keeping operations and in other NATO endeavors. Thus, while Russia will not be able to veto NATO decisions, it will be able to influence them more directly than is now the case.

Russia's Place in Europe

There is, however, a larger context to be considered: that of Russia's place in Europe. Despite all its vicissitudes, Russia is still a great power and must be recognized as such. One way of doing this, which the members of NATO are already undertaking, is to involve Russia in the work of important bodies such as the contact group that hammered out the terms of peace in Bosnia and the Group of Seven leading industrialized nations (Britain, Canada, France, Germany, Italy, Japan and the United States), which wields enormous influence over economic policies. Another way, which has captured the interest of some European members of NATO, would be to create an informal consortium of great powers including Russia, perhaps within the OSCE, perhaps outside it, by expanding the scope of the contact group. Whatever the measures adopted, Russia should be given "a seat at the table" in all the councils of Europe and in the proposed Atlantic Partnership Council.

Nowhere is the Russian presence more important than in the deliberations on, and the structures designed to underpin, the creation of a "stable, secure, integrated and undivided democratic Europe." Already Russia and the United States (presumably speaking for the other members of NATO) have agreed that the approach taken should be based on the principles of respect for human rights, democracy and political pluralism and the sovereignty and territorial integrity of all states, as set forth in various documents of the Organization for Security and Cooperation in Europe, and that they should work together to enhance the operational capability of that organization and its ability to develop a new model for security in Europe. Bringing Russia into partnership with the West may be a long and difficult endeavor, but at least the process has begun.

5

Institutional Relationships

ENTIRELY ASIDE from the Russian question, the Western allies face the problem of reconciling their own conflicting perspectives on the future security architecture of Europe. These differences do not stem from dissatisfaction with NATO, which is highly popular. Instead they derive from the changes in the geopolitical situation following the end of the cold war and the growing involvement of the European Union in security issues.

While the Soviet threat existed, the U.S. commitment and contribution to European defense were essential, and NATO was the vehicle which ensured American involvement. The changes following the end of the cold war radically reduced the threat and hence the need for such massive U.S. defense support. Moreover, the United States not only reduced its forces in Europe but seemed to some observers to "tilt away" from Europe in favor of Asia, to diverge increasingly from its European allies on issues ranging from Bosnia to the speed of expansion, and to drift toward isolationism and selective involvement in matters affecting the peace and security of the Continent. Thus, some West Europeans concluded that they should look for alternative ways to ensure their security.

The same alterations in the geopolitical situation which prompted changes in American policy also led to changes in Europe. For one, they strengthened the views of those who felt that Europe should be more than a "geographical expression," that it should evolve into a more interactive, more cooperative, more self-reliant community of states. In the field of security, that meant a Pan-European system. For another, they facilitated the process of integration of the European Union, which has developed from a primarily economic entity to one with a political role, to which it may soon add a security dimension. Thus, NATO must deal not just with beliefs that a European security organization would be a "good thing" but with the fact that the new architecture of Europe incorporates a mix of institutions with overlapping and varied memberships, which frequently have divergent interests.

To its credit, NATO, after initially trying to expand its role and extend its influence at the expense of other regional organizations, has adapted. It has recognized that the Organization for Security and Cooperation in Europe, a regional institution under Article VIII of the UN Charter with a nearly universal European membership, should be the primary instrument for monitoring crises and determining when peacekeeping operations are necessary. In fact, NATO not only agreed that peacekeeping in Europe should be carried out under the authority of the UN or the OSCE but offered to support their efforts. However, the members of NATO have not, so far, agreed to exchange liaison officers with the OSCE or to give it a role in the Partnership for Peace program. And while there are de facto guidelines—for example, the OSCE and not NATO operates on the territories of the former Soviet Union—much still needs to be done in developing the "rational allocation of tasks and missions," suggested in 1994.

There are a number of reasons for this lack of progress. One is that the OSCE would find it difficult politically to devolve some of its responsibilities to NATO or to agree to call on it for certain kinds of peacekeeping operations although it might do so on an ad hoc basis. Another is that NATO, satisfied with the progress of the PFP, sees no need to enhance the operational capabilities of the OSCE. A third is that NATO wishes to preserve not only its freedom to decide whether to respond to requests from the OSCE but its own independence of action, even without the approval of the OSCE. And while an OSCE imprimatur could be advantageous politically, seeking it will open the way to discussion, and perhaps a veto, of NATO proposals by countries such as Russia and Croatia. Thus, NATO has been chary of working too closely with the OSCE.

NATO's Relationship with the WEU

NATO has moved much further in its relationship with the Western European Union, which was asked in the Treaty of Maastricht "to elaborate and implement decisions and actions of the [European] Union...[that] have defense implications." An elegant blending of roles (and fudging of divergent national approaches) led to WEU also being accepted as the "European pillar of the alliance" and to NATO's acknowledgment that the development of a European security and defense identity by the EU could not only strengthen that pillar but could enable the European allies to take greater responsibility for their own defense. Moreover, NATO promised to help strengthen the WEU by identifying units which could be used by the European allies in pursuing their common foreign and security policy, to establish Combined Joint Task Forces which could carry out European missions and by facilitating planning for these missions and exercises for troops that would take part in them, all in the interests of developing the European Security and Defense Identity *within* NATO.

At first glance, these arrangements look like the ultimate in cooperation—and indeed they go far toward providing the WEU with military capabilities that it might not otherwise be able to acquire. On closer reading of the text, there are, however, a number of conditions that make the relationship more one of patron and client. For one, the North Atlantic Council must not only approve all the planning and training exercises but also the actual use of NATO assets. Thus, the council can, at any moment, "pull the plug." For another, the WEU in return not only recognizes that the alliance is the essential forum for consultation but indicates its "readiness to pursue common security objectives through the alliance, wherever possible," thus limiting *its* freedom of action. And for a third, it was revealed in the speeches *after* the June 1996 meeting of the North Atlantic Council, that WEU will normally be limited to humanitarian missions, aid to the civil powers, etc., and will not undertake "combat-related operations or very large-scale operations." In short, NATO is not giving away much in proffering support.

Although there will certainly be problems in the implementation of the NATO program, over the command of the European troops and the procedures for releasing NATO assets to WEU, the major difficulty may well arise with respect to the role of WEU itself. Militarily, that organization would seem to be firmly rooted in, and largely controlled by, NATO; yet it is charged with implementing decisions of the European Union that have defense implications. Given that the membership of the two organizations is different and that their security policies may be, WEU could be whipsawed between the two. Moreover, if the current intergovernmental conference decides to integrate the WEU into the EU and to move toward a common defense, further problems could arise. Though NATO control of WEU may be acceptable now as the price that has to be paid for military capabilities attainable in no other way, it may not be acceptable if and when the EU develops a more cohesive structure and gains a new sense of its role in Europe. Here, much will depend on whether that role is limited to the conduct of peacekeeping operations (as Austria, Denmark, Finland, Ireland and Sweden would hold), or whether it could include that larger military mission that other countries (notably France and Germany) deem essential to the future of the EU as a political organization. If the latter vision of the EU receives endorsement, even as a long-term objective, then the potential for differences with NATO over the development of the European Security and Defense Identity will be high indeed.

This leads directly to the question of overall NATO-EU relationships. In one sense, the two organizations perfectly complement each other, one being primarily military-political and the other primarily economic-political. Moreover, in practical ways their activities have been complementary, with the NATO-controlled Implementation Force (IFOR) providing security in the Bosnian town of Mostar and the EU administering and rebuilding that city. So far, however, that complementarity has not been utilized, either in planning for peacekeeping operations or in the larger context of promoting European security. There has, for example, been no effort to correlate admission to the EU with entry into NATO or, more importantly, to induce the EU to step up its political and economic interactions with prospective NATO members, as an adjunct to, or a substitute for, their induction into the Atlantic alliance. And as yet there has been no formal discussion of the ways in which the EU might contribute to the promotion of "Euro-Atlantic security"; in fact, the EU was not even mentioned in the communiqué issued following the NATO Ministerial Meeting of December 10, 1996.

NATO Adaptability

In sum, since 1989 NATO has made a series of adjustments in its relations with other organizations. These have varied both with the apparent need for help from different sources and with their usefulness. For instance, NATO reliance on the Organization for Security and Cooperation in Europe, as distinct from NATO's rhetorical endorsement of that institution, diminished after it proved no better than any other in devising a workable solution for Bosnia. Relations have also varied with shifts in political leadership. President Jacques Chirac of France was more inclined than his predecessor to reconsider the subject of French involvement in the Integrated Military Command Structure, and President Clinton is more accepting of the "European identity" in NATO than President George Bush.

Since both circumstances and personalities are mutable, is it possible to predict future institutional relationships? One way of doing this is to examine what is now going on. In principle, the OSCE, EU, WEU and NATO all have roles to play. In practice, NATO seems to be "poaching on their preserves." For example, the OSCE is charged with conflict prevention and crisis management; so is NATO. The WEU is concerned primarily with peacekeeping operations, but so are the participants in the NATO-sponsored Partnership for Peace. Moreover, NATO itself, and specifically the North American members, are earmarking assets for peacekeeping, along with other missions. And, as noted earlier, the subordination of the WEU to NATO ensures that the EU cannot take any significant military action in support of its common foreign and security policy unless both policy and action conform to the positions held by NATO—which is to say, by the United States. Thus, while NATO modestly describes itself as "one of the cornerstones of stability and security in Europe," its Integrated Military Command Structure, its virtual monopoly on organized military forces and its smoothly functioning decision processes that back up its broad interpretation of its mission may well make it *the* cornerstone of the security architecture of Europe.

This in itself is not necessarily bad, in that NATO fulfills a purpose that no other organization or combination of organizations can and ensures American involvement in the maintenance of security and stability in Europe. Such a role for NATO may not, however, satisfy Russian desires for a security architecture in which the Atlantic alliance plays a less dominant role or fulfill the interests of the traditionally neutral states which attach less importance to military security. A key role for NATO may, moreover, stifle the full development of the European Union, require that NATO shift its attention and its resources to fields in which its competence is less than it is in military affairs and perhaps overload it. Thus, NATO may, in its own interest, want to consider divesting itself of some of its responsibilities and helping other organizations to assume them.

6

NATO and Peacekeeping Operations

THE MOST IMMEDIATE threat facing NATO is that national rivalries, religious quarrels, class struggles or political instability may lead to internal upheavals within states, such as have occurred in Yugoslavia; to secessionist movements, as in Georgia and Moldova; or to conflicts between states, such as that between Armenia and Azerbaijan over Nagorno-Karabakh. There are some 25 current or potential flash points in Europe alone. It is possible that these conflicts could involve other states, as Russia has been involved in Georgia, and Serbia in Croatia. Thus, a primary problem for NATO is that of maintaining peace and security in its own backyard.

NATO is keenly aware of this and has sought to head off or dampen conflicts both by pressing the Organization for Security and Cooperation in Europe to take action and by itself taking on the as-yet-undefined task of crisis management. Moreover, cognizant that neither the OSCE nor the UN has troops at its disposal, NATO has indicated its willingness to support on a case-by-case basis and in accordance with its own procedures peacekeeping operations under the authority of the UN Security Council or the OSCE. The question is: What does this mean in practice?

The answer depends on the interpretation of "peacekeeping." As defined and implemented by the UN, it has involved small, lightly armed forces, whose function has been to monitor agreements reached by warring elements, which operate only with their consent and normally may use their weapons only in self-defense. This is not the kind of mission that would require sizable NATO forces. In fact, the small specialized elements from the 30-odd countries now being trained under the Partnership for Peace program would serve this purpose admirably. Though these elements might benefit from NATO's logistic backup and support, these could be made available to the "ready" force that former UN Secretary General Boutros Boutros-Ghali sought to establish or to ad hoc groupings. And, while NATO might prefer to control even minor operations in the European area, there is no reason this could not be done by the OSCE, which already has observer teams deployed in Chechnya, Georgia and Moldova, monitoring peacekeeping activities.

The problem is that "peacekeeping" as defined above does not always apply because the needs may vary, from protecting humanitarian relief assistance to providing military assistance to civilian authorities, because agreements break down or cannot be reached, in which case troops may be deployed between parties which are in conflict or on the verge of it. "Peace maintenance" may well require larger, better-armed elements than peacekeeping. The troops deployed may have to remain in place for a long time; for example, those on Cyprus have been there since 1964. And there is always the possibility that they may become involved in an Afghanistan-type conflict, of long duration and uncertain outcome, a consideration which allegedly affected the decision of the West Europeans in 1992 not to send forces to Yugoslavia.

In such cases, as illustrated by Bosnia, forces such as Unprofor (United Nations Protection Force) may well lack the command structure, the staff system and the logistical support which NATO can provide. Moreover, there is something to be said for giving one commander full responsibility for implementing the mandate of the OSCE or the UN Security Council and full authority to do so, thereby avoiding the "second-guessing" by UN officials and the bitter quarrels between them and the military leaders that undermined the effectiveness of Unprofor. There is, however, no necessity for NATO to appoint that commander, who could instead come from the WEU, under the provisions for the transfer of forces, staffs and control of operations spelled out in the Berlin Communiqué of June 1996. (Indeed, had these procedures been in effect in 1992, they might have enabled the United States to endorse and support more rigorous action in Bosnia without having to "bite the bullet" on committing ground forces. Whether their European allies would have agreed to that action absent U.S. involvement is another question.)

NATO Essential to Enforcing Peace

When, however, it comes to "peace enforcement," in the sense of major military operations against a party to a conflict that persists in aggressive actions, as the Bosnian Serbs did in August 1995, or that violates the terms of settlement, as all three of the parties to the Dayton peace accord are doing today, NATO is clearly the only effective instrument. This holds for at least two reasons: NATO alone, among European institutions, can make available the forces and the command structure needed for any significant military operation. And, unless the United States takes part, such an operation will lack both the military resources and the political backing necessary to launch it.

One problem in both peace enforcement and the more robust forms of peace maintenance is that of defining the mission of the military. Clearly, it cannot be simply that of separating combatants who disregard their presence: the inactivity of the United Nations Interim Force in Lebanon (Unifil, formed in 1975) while Israeli troops and militiamen of various loyalties pass through its lines has exacerbated the situation in that country rather than improving it. Nor can the military limit their activities to separating the warring sides if this enables war criminals to move about freely, advocates of ethnic cleansing to terrorize people who seek to live where they choose, or armed partisans of one side or another to engage in firefights in the territory controlled by those charged with maintaining the peace. Unless that mission is linked directly to the attainment of the desired political outcome, neither peace enforcement nor peace maintenance is likely to be effective

Another problem is that the members of NATO may be unwilling to support precisely those kinds of operations in which NATO military capabilities might be most useful. There are a number of reasons for this. Many breaches of the peace (such as human-rights violations on a genocidal scale) may not be seen as direct threats to security. Even where the threat is palpable, not all members may assess it identically. Their willingness to act might depend on their interest in a particular outcome, and they will undoubtedly differ in their estimates of the political and economic costs of action, especially since each government will face a different domestic situation. And while endorsement of a proposed response by the OSCE or the UN Security Council might sway some votes, this is not likely to offset their reluctance to go beyond the traditional peacekeeping mission.

Accordingly, NATO cannot be expected to conclude in advance that it will undertake peacekeeping operations if a particular threat to security materializes. Nor can all members be counted upon to participate. The best that can be hoped for is that NATO will authorize "coalitions of the willing" to utilize NATO facilities, to use (a portion of) NATO headquarters and staffs and to employ elements of their forces earmarked for NATO. Indeed, the organization of the Combined Joint Task Forces mentioned earlier is both an acknowledgment of this fact and a means of involving not only members of NATO but countries belonging to the WEU or the Partnership for Peace in future peacekeeping operations.

There are a number of unresolved issues in NATO policy on peacekeeping operations. One is *where* it will act. Although the operation in Bosnia showed that NATO is ready to send forces outside the treaty area, it does not tell us how far out. Presumably NATO will not again consider sending peacekeepers to the Caucasus, as it offered to do in 1992, but would it send them to the Baltic republics? to Moldova? to the Middle East? Another is *when* it will send them. Clearly, this will be determined by the magnitude of the requirement and the nature of the conflict. But it would be helpful to know whether large-scale operations will be undertaken only when there is a "serious threat to international security," to cite the UN Charter, or whether, as in Bosnia, these could be triggered by lesser threats or simply by long-lasting civil conflicts. A third issue is whether the decision to act will be made by NATO alone or debated in other forums. Granted that NATO will always have the right to reject or amend proposals originating elsewhere, is there not some advantage to discussing the question initially in bodies such as the proposed Atlantic Partnership Council or the Organization for Security and Cooperation in Europe, where there will be a wider range of opinions? Then there is the question of *how* the decision will be reached: by consensus or by letting those willing to act decide what to do—a common-sense approach but one which departs from past procedures. Finally, there remains the decision concerning who will carry out the proposed operation: NATO itself, the WEU using NATO assets, the OSCE or the UN, with the participation of elements from the Partnership for Peace. And though most of these questions are unlikely to be answered before the occasion that requires a decision by NATO, thinking about them in advance may help.

7

NATO's Mission
in the 'New Europe'

P RIOR TO 1989 NATO had a single military mission: to deter, and if necessary to defend against, aggression directed at one of its members, presumably by the Warsaw Treaty Organization. Its nonmilitary mission was larger, including not only promoting détente and supporting arms control but (though these were of lesser significance) encouraging economic cooperation among members of the alliance, stimulating scientific research, disseminating information about NATO, etc. Since then, the world in general, and Europe in particular, has changed drastically. What, then, should be the mission(s) of NATO in the new Europe?

Military Tasks

Deterrence of, and defense against, aggression is still a goal, but the scenario has changed. There is no longer a Warsaw Treaty Organization (nor a Soviet Union) and aggression by the largest surviving entity, Russia, is both politically unlikely and militarily implausible: an army of 700,000 men that cannot oust a few thousand lightly armed guerrillas from a town on its own territory can scarcely be taken seriously. Nor does there seem much prospect that other countries will pose significant threats to either new members or old. For example, Syria, Iraq and other neighbors of "Turkey in Asia" have no reason to attack that country, which is, moreover, stronger militarily than most of its neighbors put together. While the threat that either "rogue states" or terrorists might employ weapons of mass destruction against a member of the Atlantic alliance remains, it is by no means clear what NATO will do about it. At the moment, it is attempting to cope with this possibility by measures ranging from preventing nuclear proliferation to stepping up antiterrorist operations. Though deploying antiballistic missile (ABM) defenses remains a possibility, it is not much more than that, for reasons ranging from technical problems to recognition that nuclear weapons could readily be introduced clandestinely. Higher priority seems to be given to tactical ABMs, which could protect forces and bases, than to systems which could safeguard centers of population and industry in Europe.

For these reasons, the mission of collective defense may be more justifiable in terms of the sense of reassurance it conveys to members than for its utility as a "shield" for NATO. While this may not warrant abrogating this mission, it tends to justify the judgment made in the 1991 statement on "The Alliance's Strategic Concept" that "risks to Allied security are less likely to result from calculated aggression against the territory of the allies, but rather from the adverse consequences of instabilities..." and thus attaching to it less importance than previously.

The same cannot be said of a second military mission: crisis management, i.e., the use of troops to back up political moves. In some instances, this would involve no more than the redeployment of units to indicate resolve or to hint at further action; their use to seal off a frontier; or their employment to enforce an embargo. In other instances, however, NATO forces may be required to separate warring elements or to force them to stop fighting, i.e., to practice peacekeeping. This is, then, perhaps the most important and certainly the most urgent task of the alliance. Militarily, NATO is well prepared to carry out this mission, even if requirements exceed those of Bosnia.

56

Politically, the degree of readiness for action is more questionable and there are potentially divisive differences among members. Hence, some argue for limiting the scope of operations or transferring primary responsibility to the WEU and/or OSCE. Others propose changing the decision process within NATO, so that "coalitions of the willing" (if they can ever be formed) will not be blocked from taking action by the veto power inherent in seeking consensus. And while all agree that this change could affect the "indivisibility" of the alliance, its proponents see it as essential, despite its adverse consequences.

Access to Vital Resources

The third military mission, that of precluding disruption of the flow of vital resources, i.e., of oil from the Middle East, falls somewhere between the first two. Although disruption is unlikely, it could be dangerous to the security of Europe. Restoring the flow of oil could generate military requirements, especially for logistic support, that would be hard to meet. And there is even stronger opposition to undertaking military actions in the Middle East than there is to peacekeeping, partly because these actions are viewed as inappropriate to the objective of keeping the oil flowing, partly because allies are pursuing different national interests in the region. For example, Turkey has agreed to build a gas pipeline with Iran, despite U.S. efforts to isolate that country economically. And while "Desert Storm," the multinational response to the Iraqi invasion of Kuwait in 1990, showed that dramatic threats can trigger dramatic responses, it by no means guarantees that NATO will act on every occasion. In fact, NATO has never endorsed any of the military measures in the Middle East taken by member states.

These findings have significant implications for the future role of NATO. On the one hand, they emphasize the need for the consultative processes which are the hallmark of NATO, for the continuation of an integrated system for the command and control of troops assigned to NATO and for the maintenance by its members of the forces required to carry out its several missions. On the other hand, they argue for radical changes in the present Integrated Military Command Structure that would better fit it to conduct the smaller-scale, militarily flexible and politically sensitive operations that are most likely to take place. They argue also for a revamping of the forces that NATO asks its members to maintain, so that these are better suited to the tasks at hand. These may require augmented air-transport capabilities rather than more armored divisions.

While NATO is already embarked on this process of change, the question is whether it can escape the shibboleths of the past and the political and financial constraints of the present and meet the (admittedly not well-defined) requirements of the future.

Political Agenda

Politically, NATO is committed to "the establishment of a just and lasting peaceful order in Europe," toward which it is working in three major ways:

▸ By seeking to bring the countries of Europe into a set of relationships that would enhance their sense of security and provide a basis for dealing with future threats;

▸ By attempting to create a framework of mutually reinforcing institutions which can help to preserve peace, or to restore it when it is broken;

▸ By promoting peaceful, prosperous and stable democracies in Eastern Europe and, so far as is possible, among the states which were formerly part of the Soviet Union.

NATO has already taken steps to achieve the first objective by expanding contacts with the countries of Eastern Europe and the former Soviet Union. It has established the North Atlantic Cooperation Council (of which these countries are members); set up the Partnership for Peace and pledged to consult with any partner which feels threatened; and promised

AMMER
WIENER ZEITUNG
Vienna
AUSTRIA

Cartoonists & Writers Syndicate

membership in NATO to some of these partners. Moreover, it has promoted the Pact for Stability (under which countries that are at odds with one another agree to settle their disputes, as Hungary did with regard to its ethnic minorities in Romania'), and it has agreed to a new NATO-Russian council and is in the process of establishing an Atlantic Partnership Council which will subsume both NACC and the PFP.

It has also tried to involve other organizations in this process, for example, by encouraging the OSCE to play a larger role in preventing conflicts and managing crises and by assisting the WEU in developing military capabilities that would enable it to contribute to the maintenance of peace and security in Europe. There are, however, three points to be noted concerning the attempt to create a new security architecture of Europe. One is that while there is a plethora of institutions which can establish principles of conduct, monitor their implementation and help to defuse crises, only NATO has the capacity to restore the peace where this requires a significant military effort. A second is that the writ of all these institutions varies with the geography of Europe. In the Commonwealth of Independent

States, for example, Russia is the principal peacekeeper—as well as, some would say, the principal source of threats to the peace. And finally, NATO has not yet come up with a way to provide a "security umbrella" for those countries that may not become members of the Atlantic alliance—something which may require much closer relations with, and much greater support for, the OSCE than has so far been envisioned.

NATO has been even less successful in the third task: that of promoting peaceful, prosperous and stable democracies. This is not surprising. As economist Alan Tonelson reminds us, "military power does not readily address most of the threats to stability...for example, the serious structural economic decline in Europe, the continuing economic stagnation in the newly independent countries of Eastern Europe and the Russian near abroad, and...the growing refugee flows coming into Western Europe...." Moreover, NATO lacks most of the policy instruments which would be useful in improving stability: economic resources, financial incentives, technical assistance, adjustments of barriers to trade, etc., to say nothing of opportunities for political consultation and engagement across a much wider range of issues than security. Thus NATO must turn elsewhere, and the logical choice is the European Union.

Furthermore, the EU is better equipped to deal with non-military threats. At one level, these include crime, drugs and terrorism, all matters which are touched on in one or more drafts of the EU's common foreign and security policy. At another level, they include degradation of the environment, alterations in the ecological balance, deficiencies in the basic necessities of life and widening gaps in income levels, both within nations and between developed and developing countries. While neither the EU nor anyone else has answers to all these problems, addressing them is at least as important as maintaining the military balance in Europe, and perhaps more so.

Possible Roles for NATO

In the longer run, the mission of NATO will depend on which version of the new Europe prevails. One possibility would be that the Continent would revert to the traditional model of international politics, with nations competing for power and influence and seeking to secure their interests by forming ad hoc alliances. While such a reversal of present trends is unlikely, it could be triggered if existing institutions were unable to put an end to civil wars and/or to curb the repression of ethnic minorities; if there were a replay of efforts to redraw the map of Europe, as Serbia and Croatia attempted to do in the early 1990s; or if a future Russian government decided that it had to protect itself from the consequences of NATO expansion—which is why the scope, pace and nature of that enlargement are so important. Under such circumstances, the members of the Atlantic alliance might become increasingly concerned about protecting their own interests, by force if necessary, and NATO could become a more militarized, if not a more interventionist, organization. Gone by the board would be the present emphasis on establishing a comprehensive security framework, promoting democracy and supporting economic growth and social progress in other countries, and with them the possibility of reversing the process described above.

A 'Europe of States'?

Another scenario would be one in which a "Europe of states" avoided the pitfalls described above and continued to collaborate in institutions such as NATO and the OSCE, and perhaps outside them, in a NATO-Russia or NATO-Commonwealth of Independent States council. Hopefully, the EU would continue to flourish. The countries of Europe would not, however, establish an overarching arrangement for promoting either economic integration or security. In this context, NATO would essentially play the role it now does, emphasizing crisis management.

A "Europe whole and free," to borrow the felicitous phrase of Ambassador James Goodby, a long-time negotiator on issues of European security, would imply enormous political, economic and social progress on the part of new or newly emerging states; a sharp diminution in conflicts within or among these states; and an architecture of Europe which could build on a revised and strengthened OSCE, with or without a "directorate of great powers." If this came about, NATO's importance and influence would be vastly diminished and it might skeletonize or dissolve its military structure, relying on the political commitments under Articles 4 and 5 of the NATO treaty to deter any threats to security.

Another possibility would be the emergence of a new and more Westernized Europe centered around a larger and stronger EU that could further extend its reach by negotiating treaties of association with nonmembers. Although the EU is unlikely, barring either an American disengagement in Europe or the assertion of a European identity, to develop significant military capabilities, it could assume primary responsibility for all aspects of preserving the peace, ranging from promoting civic harmony to separating hostile elements. Devolving this mission on the countries of Europe would be a step toward making them more responsible for the security of the region in which they are located, within the framework of the transatlantic partnership, in cooperation with a NATO which still had the task of deterring or coping with possible aggression.

Cooperation between NATO and the EU on matters relating to the security of Europe could, moreover, facilitate the next move, the formation of a transatlantic cooperation community. The German defense minister, Volker Ruhe, called for "a new, wider transatlantic contract" that would enhance cooperation on behalf of Western economic interests and democratic values. French Foreign Minister Alain Juppé has advocated "a new transatlantic charter to consolidate the common desire of North America and Europe to contribute to international stability in all its dimensions." And Malcolm Rifkind, then British defense minister, capped the discussion at the 1995 Wehrkunde Conference in Munich, Germany, by noting that "defense issues alone do not offer a broad enough foundation for the edifice we need"—a statement which is perhaps a fitting end to a discussion of the future role of NATO.

8

The United States and NATO

U.S. POLICY toward NATO must be viewed in the context of U.S. policy toward the larger world. By and large, the United States seeks to enhance its own security, to promote global and regional stability, to further the spread of democracy and the growth of market economies, and to foster an open international trading system that can in turn help to stimulate the domestic economy: in other words, it wants to shape the world to its liking. In so doing, it seeks to enlist the political, economic and military support of friends and allies, both for the furtherance of peaceful aims and as a hedge against the possibility of war. And it both presumes and assumes a position of leadership in all these areas, a role which it sought to play even before it became the only superpower in the world. Obviously, then, the United States has global interests and must operate on a global basis.

Europe, however, is still a vital area, if not the vital area, of the globe, since it is home to many of the world's democracies, to a large number of advanced industrial societies (including four of the members of the Group of Seven), to a cluster of trading/investment partners and to most of America's important allies. The United States has, therefore, a great stake in maintaining its influence over the decisions and policies of European governments and multinational organizations. NATO is important not only because it assists in promoting the peace and security that are an essential underpinning to economic progress in Europe but because through it the United States can influence the policies of members in other areas.

Given its economic strength, military capabilities, scale of contributions to the Atlantic alliance and long history of leadership, it is clear that the United States will have a major influence on NATO's future role—in fact, on its continued existence. What is less clear is what the United States will ask of NATO, partly because some of this country's current policies are inherently contradictory, partly because, in the American form of government, different elements can influence policy, and partly because public opinion is divided on some of the issues facing NATO and ambivalent about others.

All of these factors impinge on the policy of the Clinton Administration with respect to NATO enlargement. As indicated earlier, the United States has been one of the strongest proponents of expansion, which it sees as a means of enhancing peace and security in Eastern Europe and of ending the division of Europe—objectives which seemingly have wide popular support in America. However, the emphasis in NATO communiqués on security guarantees, together with the insistence on freedom to deploy forces on the territory of new members if the situation requires it, is difficult to explain (especially to the Russians) if the objective is enhancing security for all. Moreover, the rationale for enlargement given by some supporters is not that of "strengthening security in the entire region" but, as Senator John McCain (R-Ariz.) said, to "make irreversible the outcome of 1989" by emphasizing to Russia "that these states are not now in nor will they return to a Russian sphere of influence."

The U.S. proposal to admit to NATO all countries that qualify for membership seems to have support among the American people, who in opinion polls conducted in 1996 favored admitting nine nations (including Russia) but were divided on "risking lives" to defend new members from attack. However, the question of which countries to admit, and when, is just now entering the consciousness of the American people, over two thirds of whom indicated in one survey done in 1996 that they knew "not very much" or "nothing at all" about the subject. Thus, the Administration may need to make a more persuasive case for enlargement if it is to secure the necessary support.

Administration Policy Toward Russia

One element that will affect the outcome is American policy toward Russia. So far, the policy of the Clinton Administration has been to attempt to bring Russia into the "new Europe" by providing economic and technical assistance; trying to promote Russian partnership in various Western-oriented organizations; engaging in various forms of military cooperation; and endeavoring to work out an agreement between Russia and NATO that would provide for consultations on issues affecting European security, mutual guarantees of peaceful relations, and the establishment of a NATO-Russian council. Although the questions asked did not go into this detail, a majority of those polled in one 1996 survey favored pacing NATO expansion in ways that would accommodate Russian concerns (a policy also favored by Senator Sam Nunn (D-Ga.), former chairman of the Senate Armed Services Committee) and even admitting Russia as a member. Moreover, while over 60 percent judged that enlargement would place NATO in a stronger position if Russia should become aggressive, a similar percentage did not deem Russia "aggressive by nature." In contrast, others do regard Russia as a potential adversary or, while not going that far, would agree with Senator Richard Lugar (R-Ind.) that "Russia is not a partner.... [I]t is a very serious and tough rival." Still others are persuaded that Russia should not be rewarded for what they regard as unacceptable behavior, both in the near abroad and in Chechnya. The fact that the Clinton Administration is seemingly doing so gave some political opponents the opportunity to castigate the Administration as "soft on Russia." Here, again, the U.S. government may need to make a more persuasive case for the policy it is pursuing, perhaps by emphasizing that failure to tie Russia closely to the West could result in a new division of Europe and a consequent requirement for a larger, and more expensive, military contribution to NATO.

The Administration policy with respect to institutional relations is very clear: NATO is the most important entity and should be the keystone of the architecture of Europe. This means that the United States wants the security policy of the European Union to complement alliance policy and the Western European Union to act in conformity with the positions adopted in NATO. Within that context, the Clinton Administration is much readier than its predecessors to accept the push for a European security and defense identity; to assist in developing that identity (within NATO); and to recognize that this may change both the structure of NATO and the process of decisionmaking. Apparently, the price paid may be worth it if the end result is a Europe which truly serves as a pillar of the Atlantic alliance, with all that implies in terms both of policy coordination and burden-sharing. Some aspects of this approach, notably attaching primacy to NATO and increasing the share of defense responsibilities (and costs) borne by the Europeans, would receive support across the entire political spectrum. Many would, however, argue for an even greater emphasis on U.S. leadership in NATO and look askance at what could be considered power-sharing by the United States. Thus, the government may be constrained on how far—and how fast—it can go in reshaping NATO or in devising a framework for European security that would diminish the role and the importance of the United States.

The issue that has aroused the most contention, inside and outside the U.S. government, is, however, that of U.S. participation in peacekeeping operations. On the one hand, the Clinton Administration has accepted the 1992 decision of the North Atlantic Council to consider requests by the UN or the OSCE to support peacekeeping operations and strongly backed the creation of the Partnership for Peace, one instrument for responding to such requests. On the other hand, it has set stiff conditions for participation and even stiffer ones for involvement in Bosnia, the one operation that has come before NATO.

Opposition to a U.S. Peacekeeping Role

The U.S. military mission to protect aid operations in Somalia in 1993 (which cost 18 American lives) had a strong effect on U.S. public opinion and hence on the willingness of the Clinton Administration again to risk such outcomes. This failure, the costly 1994–95 military intervention in Haiti to restore the democratically elected president, Jean-Bertrand Aristide, and the long stalemate in Yugoslavia generated political opposition, which in some instances cut across party lines, to involvement in UN peacekeeping efforts. (Even though former President George Bush had offered in 1992 to train U.S. forces for peacekeeping operations, it was another Republican, Senator Bob Dole (Kans.), who charged in 1995 that "the American people will not tolerate American casualties for irresponsible internationalism.") Moreover, the U.S. military were reluctant to take part in any peacekeeping operations, which they saw as a diversion from their primary mission of deterring or fighting wars and a depletion of the resources available for that mission. Their views were shared by many outside the armed forces. It is, therefore, no wonder that Anthony Lake, former national security adviser to President Clinton, wrote that "peacekeeping is not at the center of our [American] foreign or defense policy."

These divergences over peacekeeping operations extend to other aspects of NATO's mission and to that of American forces in Europe. At the moment, the United States maintains in Europe (at a direct cost of some $10 billion per year) two army divisions, one fighter wing and one air transport wing. Additionally, the powerful U.S. Sixth Fleet is deployed in the Mediterranean. These forces serve to demonstrate the U.S. interest in Europe and to underpin the U.S. commitment to NATO, on whose importance all elements seemingly agree. Where the differences arise is over what the Allied forces should do. The

Clinton Administration argues that "meeting the new kinds of challenge…is the task on which NATO adaptation must chiefly focus." At the same time, it is highly selective with respect to the tasks it endorses, showing limited enthusiasm for peacekeeping and a perhaps unrealistic desire to enlist the European allies in U.S.-led military operations in the Middle East. Conversely, critics of Administration policy, in and out of political life, seem to be looking more toward a NATO focused on its traditional mission of collective defense than to one which would emphasize new military tasks, even though some of them acknowledge that "Europe currently faces no clear and present danger from any major power."

Opinion about the longer-term mission of NATO is not so much divided as unformed. A majority of those queried in September 1996 supported transforming NATO into a more inclusive and diverse security system. However, those holding this view apparently did not consider the form that the new NATO should take or its ability to carry out the missions they did deem important, such as coping with terrorism and the spread of weapons of mass destruction, dealing with threats arising outside Europe, such as the Persian Gulf war of 1991, and conducting peacekeeping operations in the areas surrounding NATO territory. Some analysts have favored a "division of labor" in which the Western European Union would take greater responsibility for European security and the United States would act only when its military contribution would be unique or could be decisive. However, this approach has been little discussed outside of think tanks. And though the U.S. Department of State has endorsed a "New Atlantic Community" in which a revised NATO would work with other institutions to preserve the peace, to promote European integration and to enhance transatlantic cooperation, it emphasizes that Americans are not "making a clone of the West as we have known it…[but] are engaged in the exciting process of inventing our community…." Thus, the United States has the opportunity to make the choices about, and influence the decisions on, the future role of NATO.

Talking It Over

A Note for Students and Discussion Groups

This issue of the HEADLINE SERIES, like its predecessors, is published for every serious reader, specialized or not, who takes an interest in the subject. Many of our readers will be in classrooms, seminars or community discussion groups. Particularly with them in mind, we present below some discussion questions—suggested as a starting point only—and references for further reading.

Discussion Questions

Like most alliances, NATO was formed to cope with the threat of armed attack. That threat has virtually vanished. Does this mean that NATO should vanish also? If not, why not?

If NATO does continue, what role should it play? "Defender-in-waiting" for a possible attack? Peacekeeper in Europe? Protector of Allied interests outside Europe? Or should it evolve into a multinational organization concerned primarily with maintaining peaceful relations among its members and helping to ensure their stability?

Should NATO expand? If so, how far, and in what directions? Should it extend to the Baltic republics? Ukraine? Georgia? Russia itself? And what about the Asian republics of the former Soviet Union, such as Kazakhstan and Turkmenistan? Is membership in NATO the best way of ensuring Russian cooperation in building the "new Europe" or is that the equivalent of "putting the bear in the henhouse"? If not membership, what about a "charter of association" with NATO? Or is Russia *the* adversary against which NATO should be prepared to act and which therefore should be kept at arm's length?

How can NATO enlist the European Union in the task of creating a peaceful and secure Europe? By promoting its expansion, in conjunction with, or even in lieu of, NATO enlargement? By asking it to have the Western European Union take over certain missions, such as peacekeeping? By working out a "division of labor"?

What benefits does the United States get from NATO membership that warrant the costs and the burdens? Is the payoff likely to increase or diminish in coming years? What does this imply for continued U.S. support for NATO?

The Democrats and the Republicans seem to differ sharply over NATO. The former view it as an increasingly political organization whose long-term mission is collective security and the latter see it as a largely military alliance whose primary mission is cooperative defense. Which of these approaches would you support? Why? Do you see any possibility of devising a future role on which both parties would agree?

Annotated Reading List

Bertram, Christoph, *Europe in the Balance: Securing the Peace Won in the Cold War*. Washington, DC, The Brookings Institution, 1995. An overview by a European expert of the issues confronting Europeans (and Americans) as they look toward the twenty-first century.

Drew, S. Nelson, *NATO: From Berlin to Bosnia*. McNair Paper 35. Washington, DC, Institute for National Strategic Studies, National Defense University, January 1995. A good, brief survey of the issues confronting NATO. Available for sale by the U.S. Government Printing Office (USGPO), Superintendent of Documents, Mail Stop: Washington, DC 20402-9328.

van Heuven, Marten H. A., *Russia, the United States and NATO: The Outlook for European Security*. Washington, DC, The Atlantic Council of the

United States, November 1994. A brief but useful assessment of possible roles for the major actors in the post-cold-war era. Somewhat skewed toward the U.S. position but does consider difficulties in implementing it.

Jopp, Mathias, *The Strategic Implications of European Integration*. Adelphi Paper 290. London, The International Institute for Strategic Studies, July 1994. An exhaustive analysis of the possible effects of integration on intercountry relations, on peace and security in Europe and on the roles of different organizations in bringing this about.

NATO Handbook, 1995. NATO Office of Information and Press, 110 Brussels, Belgium. Free. An invaluable reference, the handbook gives both factual information and succinct summaries of official NATO views on, and positions with respect to, the issues confronting the organization.

Office of International Security Affairs, Department of Defense, *United States Security Strategy for Europe and NATO*. Washington, DC, USGPO, June 1995. A good, comprehensive, official statement of U.S. policy as of mid-1995; somewhat dated with respect to Bosnia, but otherwise still useful.

Oppenheimer, Michael F., *Alternative Visions of the New Europe*. Occasional Paper 1995/#11. New York, American Council on Germany, 14 East 60th St., NY, NY 10022. (Complimentary copies available.) A discussion of the kinds of futures envisioned by Atlanticists, Europeanists, "Continentalists" and those espousing a "Europe of States," showing the beliefs and assumptions that underlie their differing proposals.

Papacosma, S. Victor, and Heiss, Mary Ann, eds., *NATO in the Post Cold-War Era: Does It Have a Future?* New York, St. Martin's Press, 1995. A good collection of pieces on everything from the origins of NATO to the Partnership for Peace, by authors who would generally answer yes to the question in the title.

Sloan, Stanley R., *NATO's Future: Beyond Collective Defense*. McNair Paper 46. Washington, DC, Institute for National Strategic Studies, National Defense University, December 1995. A brief but complete assessment of the issues confronting NATO and its options for the future by one of the leading experts in the field. Available for sale by the USGPO.

Thompson, Kenneth W., ed., *NATO and the Changing World Order: An Appraisal by Scholars and Policymakers*. Lanham, MD., University Press of America, 1996. A collection of lectures given in a two-year period, notable for featuring a number of critical analyses of, and dissenting views concerning, the future of NATO. The questions and answers give particularly good insights.

UNITED STATES POSTAL SERVICE™

Statement of Ownership, Management, and Circulation
(Required by 39 USC 3685)

1. Publication Title	2. Publication Number	3. Filing Date
Headline Series	0 1 1 1 - 9 8 1	April 15, 1997

4. Issue Frequency	5. Number of Issues Published Annually	6. Annual Subscription Price
Quarterly - Winter, Spring, Fall, Summer	4	$20

7. Complete Mailing Address of Known Office of Publication *(Not printer) (Street, city, county, state, and ZIP+4)*

Foreign Policy Association
470 Park Avenue South, 2nd Floor, NY, NY 10016-6819

Contact Person: Sue White
Telephone: 212/481-8100

8. Complete Mailing Address of Headquarters or General Business Office of Publisher *(Not printer)*

Same As Above

9. Full Names and Complete Mailing Addresses of Publisher, Editor, and Managing Editor *(Do not leave blank)*

Publisher *(Name and complete mailing address)*
Foreign Policy Association
470 Park Avenue South, 2nd Floor, NY, NY 10016-6819

Editor *(Name and complete mailing address)*
Nancy Hoepli-Phalon
470 Park Avenue South, 2nd Floor, NY, NY 10016-6819

Managing Editor *(Name and complete mailing address)*
N/A

10. Owner *(Do not leave blank. If the publication is owned by a corporation, give the name and address of the corporation immediately followed by the names and addresses of all stockholders owning or holding 1 percent or more of the total amount of stock. If not owned by a corporation, give the names and addresses of the individual owners. If owned by a partnership or other unincorporated firm, give its name and address as well as those of each individual owner. If the publication is published by a nonprofit organization, give its name and address.)*

Full Name	Complete Mailing Address
Foreign Policy Association	470 Park Avenue South, 2nd Floor NY, NY 10016

11. Known Bondholders, Mortgagees, and Other Security Holders Owning or Holding 1 Percent or More of Total Amount of Bonds, Mortgages, or Other Securities. If none, check box. ☑ None

Full Name	Complete Mailing Address
N/A	

12. Tax Status *(For completion by nonprofit organizations authorized to mail at special rates) (Check one)*
The purpose, function, and nonprofit status of this organization and the exempt status for federal income tax purposes:
☑ Has Not Changed During Preceding 12 Months
☐ Has Changed During Preceding 12 Months *(Publisher must submit explanation of change with this statement)*

PS Form 3526, September 1995 *(See Instructions on Reverse)*

---

13. Publication Title	14. Issue Date for Circulation Data Below
Headline Series	Spring 1997

15.	Extent and Nature of Circulation	Average No. Copies Each Issue During Preceding 12 Months	Actual No. Copies of Single Issue Published Nearest to Filing Date
a.	Total Number of Copies *(Net press run)*	8000	8000
b. Paid and/or Requested Circulation	(1) Sales Through Dealers and Carriers, Street Vendors, and Counter Sales *(Not mailed)*	778	600
	(2) Paid or Requested Mail Subscriptions *(Include advertiser's proof copies and exchange copies)*	1650	1600
c.	Total Paid and/or Requested Circulation *(Sum of 15b(1) and 15b(2))* ▶	2428	2200
d. Free Distribution by Mail *(Samples, complimentary, and other free)*		1000	950
e.	Free Distribution Outside the Mail *(Carriers or other means)*	0	0
f.	Total Free Distribution *(Sum of 15d and 15e)* ▶	1000	950
g.	Total Distribution *(Sum of 15c and 15f)* ▶	3428	3150
h. Copies not Distributed	(1) Office Use, Leftovers, Spoiled	4572	4850
	(2) Returns from News Agents	0	0
i.	Total *(Sum of 15g, 15h(1), and 15h(2))* ▶	8000	8000
	Percent Paid and/or Requested Circulation *(15c / 15g x 100)*	73%	76%

16. Publication of Statement of Ownership
☑ Publication required. Will be printed in the ___Spring___ issue of this publication.
☐ Publication not required.

17. Signature and Title of Editor, Publisher, Business Manager, or Owner

Sue White, Dir. of Finance

Date 4/15/97

I certify that all information furnished on this form is true and complete. I understand that anyone who furnishes false or misleading information on this form or who omits material or information requested on the form may be subject to criminal sanctions (including fines and imprisonment) and/or civil sanctions (including multiple damages and civil penalties).

Instructions to Publishers

1. Complete and file one copy of this form with your postmaster annually on or before October 1. Keep a copy of the completed form for your records.

2. In cases where the stockholder or security holder is a trustee, include in items 10 and 11 the name of the person or corporation for whom the trustee is acting. Also include the names and addresses of individuals who are stockholders who own or hold 1 percent or more of the total amount of bonds, mortgages, or other securities of the publishing corporation. In item 11, if none, check the box. Use blank sheets if more space is required.

3. Be sure to furnish all circulation information called for in item 15. Free circulation must be shown in items 15d, e, and f.

4. If the publication had second-class authorization as a general or requester publication, this Statement of Ownership, Management, and Circulation must be published; it must be printed in any issue in October or, if the publication is not published during October, the first issue printed after October.

5. In item 16, indicate the date of the issue in which this Statement of Ownership will be published.

6. Item 17 must be signed.

Failure to file or publish a statement of ownership may lead to suspension of second-class authorization.

PS Form 3526, September 1995 *(Reverse)*